Giving and Receiving Hospitality

[Young Children]

Other Hospitality titles in the Faith Practices® series

Giving and Receiving Hospitality [Adults] by Ted Huffman
Giving and Receiving Hospitality [Daily Life]
by Martha Brunell
Giving and Receiving Hospitality [Multiage] by Barbra Hardy
Giving and Receiving Hospitality [Older Children]
by Sandi Hannigan Marr
Giving and Receiving Hospitality [Older Youth]
by Karen Wagner
Giving and Receiving Hospitality [New Church Participants]
by Barbara Rathbun
Giving and Receiving Hospitality [Worship, Music, and Arts]
by Art Clyde
Giving and Receiving Hospitality [Young Adults]
by R.M. Keelan Downton
Giving and Receiving Hospitality [Youth]
by Lori Keller Schroeder

Other Faith Practices® for Adults

Keeping Sabbath [Young Children] by Carol Wilson
Living Stewardship [Young Children] by Linda Marsh
Playing and Living Joyfully [Young Children] by Susan Chesley

Giving and Receiving Hospitality

[Young Children]

Donna Hanby

Hampshire, England
Cleveland, Ohio

© 2010 by Circle Books.

This book edition is a licensed adaption and condensation of Faith Practices® on-line program for groups, published by The Pilgrim Press, Cleveland, Ohio. To utilize those fuller materials, which include leader instructions and group activities, please see www.FaithPractices.org.

All requests for permission to use extracts from the text version that appears in this book, please contact The Pilgrim Press at permissions@ThePilgrimPress.com or see www.ThePilgrimPress.com.

For more titles in this series, see www.Circle-Books.com.

New Revised Standard Version Bible, © 1989, Division of Christian Education of the National Council of the Churches of Christ in the United States of America. Used by permission. All rights reserved.

Faith Practices® and The Pilgrim Press® are registered trademarks and are used by permission.
CIP to come.

ISBN: 978 1 84694 490 1

Design: Stuart Davies

Printed in the UK by CPI Antony Rowe
Printed in the USA by Offset Paperback Mfrs, Inc

We operate a distinctive and ethical publishing philosophy in all areas of its business, from its global network of authors to production and worldwide distribution.

CONTENTS

Introduction: Forming Community by Giving and Receiving Hospitality   7

1. Discovery   13

2. Scripture   25

3. Discipleship   39

4. Christian Tradition   47

5. Context and Mission   67

6. Future and Vision   81

Appendix: About Faith Practices   93

Introduction

Forming Community by Giving and Receiving Hospitality

Hospitality begins with the awareness that another person, even one I think I know well, remains a stranger to me. That other person may be like me, but something always remains different from me. How, then, can we form deep meaningful community? How can strangers be welcomed into a community?

This book focuses on the Christian practice of hospitality — welcoming others into a community of giving and receiving. Seeing Christ's presence in all others enables us to welcome them as Christ into the midst of the community. As followers of Jesus, each community comes with all of the costs and joys of discipleship.

Gentle, attentive, potent, and consistent care is required to create a community where members are intentional about seeking and welcoming all, especially those whose abilities, experiences, and cultural traditions are different from the mainstream of the current community. A community of hospitality is aware, sensitive, and open to divergent cultural practices. It reaches far beyond the limits of the familiar in a highly mobile world, transforming both the newcomer and the established community.

Written for Young Children

This book is written for adults working with young children (ages 3-7) and will help lead both children and adults into new experiences of faith. Many studies demonstrate that young children have significant faith. These children are often most ready to practice the faith with us, to participate in our rituals, to engage us in loving and caring ways. Practice activities for these children assume that they have not yet developed reading skills.

Outline for This Practice

This book explores the practice from six different perspectives. Discovery introduces the practice. Scripture grounds the practice in two central texts, but each chapter begins with additional two scriptures. Discipleship seeks to follow the practices of Jesus. Tradition looks to our ancestors in the faith have understood this practice. In the Context and Mission chapter we consider ways to practice faith in our community and world. In the Vision and the Future chapter, we work on refining the practice—getting it better.

Discovery
In this Exploration we encounter the practice and explore how it intersects with human needs in community and personal life. For those for whom the particular practice is a new concept, the activities offer ways to "get to know" what it is all about. For those who have had more experience with the practice, the activities present a time of storytelling about their experiences and reflection on the impact of the practice in their lives, in the life of the church, and in the world.

Scripture
Christian faith practices grow out of the biblical story of the people of faith. For each faith practice, twelve Bible stories (two for each Exploration) inform and give direction to practicing our faith. One of these Bible stories, the *compass story*, is a guiding story out of which the faith practice grows. In the Scripture Exploration we study this story and see how it relates to all the Bible stories selected for the practice. In addition, *Faith Practices*

provides connections to Bible stories found in the Revised Common Lectionary used by many congregations in worship.

Discipleship
Discipleship is about following. Just as navigators follow a star, whether in the northern or southern hemisphere, we follow Jesus, the leader of our faith. In the Discipleship Exploration we consider what prompts people of faith to become disciples and probe how the Spirit leads us in the communal life of the Christian community and in our personal lives in the world.

Christian Tradition
Practices of faith have been shaped by those who have preceded us in the history of the Christian Church. The future will be shaped by the way we practice our faith today. Just as a map provides the landmarks we need to follow when we navigate in the world, this rich history of the Christian tradition guides us as we practice our faith today. In the Christian Tradition Exploration we seek to make the resources of the church available to those who practice faith today.

Context and Mission
In order to claim a role in the mission God gives to the church, you have to know where you are, your local context. Just as modern global positioning systems (GPS) help locate us in the world and guide us to a destination, so we need to know both the needs and realities of our local community and the direction for ministry that God gives us and the church. In the Context and Mission Exploration we consider ways to practice faith in our community and world.

Vision and the Future
Practicing our faith leads us into the future. Sometimes we need to gaze through a telescope to see the distant point to which we

are headed. Sometimes we need to peer through a microscope to see the details that are not clear to us with our normal vision. We seek to move into the future with a vision of where we are headed. In Vision and the Future exploration we consider what impels us into the future. We know that we are still practicing our faith; we won't do it perfectly. We are empowered to keep practicing.

Kinds of Activities

Each chapter can be probed through two or three different kinds of activities. These are the things we do, ways we live out each practice that helps us move into doing our faith with more depth, experience, and understanding.

Exploring and Engaging
Whether we are new to a particular faith practice or an old hand with much experience, all of us benefit from new opportunities to explore the shape of the faith practice and to engage the issues of faith that the practice offers. Sometimes this is a matter of learning new ideas about the practice. Sometimes this is more about reflecting on what we have done in our practice. The activities in Exploring and Engaging help us figure out how a faith practice intersects with our life and the life of the community of faith.

Discerning and Deciding
Practicing our faith always involves discernment: naming the realities of our community and world, and seeking the will of God for our lives and for the world. We then decide how we will act, what we will do, what values move us forward, what faith has called us to do. The activities of this type give us opportunity to practice by discerning and deciding.

Sending and Serving

Practicing our faith involves serving others and being sent out as empowered disciples of Jesus Christ. We need time in our exploration to plan how we will serve. We need moments that send us forth blessed by the community from which we venture out. These activities offer opportunities to practice our faith through sending and serving.

Helps for the Journey

I used several art elements while writing this book in the Faith Practices® series, and writers of other components used these same resources. You might find them helpful as part of your meditation or reflection. Several of these are available at www.allposters.com.

The Peaceable Kingdom by John August Swanson
The Public Fountain by Manuel Alvarez Bravo
Embrace of Peace by George Tooker
Barber Shop by Jacob Lawrence
The Luncheon of the Boating Party by Pierre-Auguste Renoir
Vendedora De Pinas by Diego Riveria

Below are some music selections that also might be helpful.

Come All You People, Tune: Uyai Mose (Iona Community)

Wade in the Water, Tune: African-American Traditional (available on internet)

Won't You Let Me Be Your Servant, Tune: Servant Song (pipe organ melody, no words, is available at www.UCCresources.com)

1

Discovery

Bible Focus Passages

Luke 19:1-10
He entered Jericho and was passing through it. A man was there named Zacchaeus; he was a chief tax collector and was rich. He was trying to see who Jesus was, but on account of the crowd he could not, because he was short in stature. So he ran ahead and climbed a sycamore tree to see him, because he was going to pass that way. When Jesus came to the place, he looked up and said to him, "Zacchaeus, hurry and come down; for I must stay at your house today." So he hurried down and was happy to welcome him. All who saw it began to grumble and said, "He has gone to be the guest of one who is a sinner." Zacchaeus stood there and said to the Lord, "Look, half of my possessions, Lord, I will give to the poor; and if I have defrauded anyone of anything, I will pay back four times as much." Then Jesus said to him, "Today salvation has come to this house, because he too is a son of Abraham. For the Son of Man came to seek out and to save the lost."

Hebrews 13:1-8, 15-16
Let mutual love continue. Do not neglect to show hospitality to strangers, for by doing that some have entertained angels without knowing it. Remember those who are in prison, as though you were in prison with them; those who are being tortured, as though you yourselves were being tortured. Let marriage be held in honor by all, and let the marriage bed be kept undefiled; for God will judge fornicators and adulterers.

Keep your lives free from the love of money, and be content with what you have; for he has said, "I will never leave you or forsake you." So we can say with confidence, "The Lord is my helper; I will not be afraid. What can anyone do to me?" Remember your leaders, those who spoke the word of God to you; consider the outcome of their way of life, and imitate their faith. Jesus Christ is the same yesterday and today and forever. .... Through him, then, let us continually offer a sacrifice of praise to God, that is, the fruit of lips that confess his name. Do not neglect to do good and to share what you have, for such sacrifices are pleasing to God.

About This Exploration

To be welcoming (hospitable), we need to care for each person and all people together. Each person has hopes, dreams, fears, and needs. Because God welcomes us into God's family, we need to welcome everyone as well. Sometimes this can be difficult, like when others do not share.

Adults put this another way. Hospitality requires expansion and adjustment of the physical and interior spaces of individuals. To be truly hospitable, individuals need to be personally centered in God's grace for themselves and others. While respecting boundaries, hospitality requires suspending territories, prejudices and judgment to establish welcome space for all. Hospitality is a radical broadening of individual worldview to welcome people outside of current experience. Receiving hospitality can be more challenging than offering it. Hospitality needs to be experienced, modeled, and practiced as a continuing expression of faith.

Description of Bible Focus Passages
Several elements of the Luke passage will appeal to children. First, they understand what it is like to have to get up on

something in order to be able to see. Second, they enjoy being selected for something special. And third, when they see someone in need, they are able to give generously just as Jesus saw that Zacchaeus was in need.

Children need consistency so they will appreciate Hebrews 13:5b and 8. If they have experienced a lot of change in their lives, then they may have trouble believing it. Verse 16 is one they may have heard in many settings and versions, but finding out that it is in the Bible may be a revelation to them.

Deep and Wide

This book is aimed at persons who are working with younger children ages 3-7. At this age there will be a wide variety of abilities among the children. Some are just beginning to recognize their name in print while others merely scribble to make drawings and pictures. Overall, their attention span is anywhere from a few minutes to fifteen minutes. You will find that most children in this age group enjoy activities with body motions, rhythm and tactile experiences. Since the age range is broad you might find that the younger children will have a hard time focusing while older learners are moving towards independence and desire to be treated as more mature.

As you prepare for this session, pray for the children who will be in your group and for yourself. Pray that God would give you patience and an eager heart to teach the children. Prepare your space to make it welcoming to young children. Include a worship/story area with either a carpet or rug to sit on, or cushions and pillows, or small chairs designed for young children.

Prayer

Gracious God, thank you for bringing me to this group of children. Help me to reflect the love You have for us so that they will feel Your presence in their lives. Amen.

The Practices

You may want to scan the list of practices before choosing any. Doing all activities in a sphere could take 90-120 minutes. Remember that young children will not be able to focus on an activity for very long. Plan more activities than you think you might need. You can always use your plan later.

Exploring and Engaging

1. Group Covenant

Read Hebrews 13:1-8, 15-16 and spend time thinking about how children in this age group can show hospitality to one another and to you as the group leader.

Gather the children in your story/worship area and tape up pieces of paper at their eye level. Ask the children about ways to make others feel welcome and how to treat others when you are in your group. Write their ideas on one sheet of the paper.

Many of the children in your group will not be able to read, but seeing the letters and hearing you say the words helps them develop pre-reading skills. You may have to encourage them to include things such as "listening when others are talking," "helping others," and "sharing." Have everyone stand up, stretch, turn around, shake hands with one another, and sit back down.

Explain that a covenant is like a promise. As a group you are going to write a covenant about how you treat one another when you are together. Read the Hebrews passage to them and have them repeat verses 1, 2 and 16 after you. Tell them that this is how God wants us to act.

Now help them to choose 5 or 6 of their ideas from the list on the paper and write them on another sheet of paper that you titled "Our Covenant." Invite the children to decorate the borders of the paper.

2. Zacchaeus Play

Read the story of Zacchaeus in Luke 19:1-5 to the children and review using the following or similar questions:

* How tall do you think Zacchaeus was?
* What did Zacchaeus do so that he could see Jesus?
* What did Jesus say to Zacchaeus?
* What did Zacchaeus tell Jesus he would do?

Line up the children from shortest to tallest. Ask the shortest child to pretend to be Zacchaeus and the tallest to pretend to be Jesus. The other children will stay in line as the crowd. Place the step stool behind one end of the line of children—maybe that child would like to pretend to be a tree and hold a few paper leaves. Have the children act out the story. Depending on the height range in your group, "Zacchaeus" may have to crouch behind the line of children. If your group is small, you may need to extend your crowd line by using chairs. Have the children act out the story including having Zacchaeus sharing his money with the poor. Continue to act out the story until every child has had the chance to be either Zacchaeus or Jesus.

3. "Zacchaeus Was a Wee Little Man" Song

Before you start the activity, review the words, music and actions for the song "Zacchaeus Was a Wee Little Man." Feel free to make up actions for the children to perform while singing. The lyrics are as follows:

> Zacchaeus was a wee little man,
> A wee little man was he,
> He climbed up in a sycamore tree
> For the Lord he wanted to see:
> And as the Savior passed him by
> He looked up in the tree,

And He said: "Zacchaeus, you come down,
For I'm going to your house today,
I'm going to your house to pray.

If you have a small group or need help in singing the song, review and cue up one or more of these renditions:

http://www.youtube.com/watch?v=S8MJDgVwOkU
http://www.youtube.com/watch?v=VCXEVtZbxQA
http://www.youtube.com/watch?v=l3yIA_h7SC0
http://www.youtube.com/watch?v=ONmBtgkP8jU
http://www.youtube.com/watch?v=nLr-lIjZciI

Gather the children in a circle and review the story of Zacchaeus. Play the music or sing the song for the children and show them the actions to go with it. Repeat the song several times. You might vary it by singing fast or slow, in a whisper or with deep voices.

Discerning and Deciding

4. Jesus Loves Me
Locate the words and music for the song "Jesus Loves Me." While many people know the first verse, there are actually 2 additional verses. Also try and locate pictures of Jesus interacting with children. Children's Bible's and the Internet can be helpful places to find the pictures. As with activity 3, if you need a larger group or help with the music, you might review and consider playing one of the following on a computer:

http://www.youtube.com/watch?v=0DYDvyBKZJA
http://www.youtube.com/watch?v=LU3xatin1yY
http://www.youtube.com/watch?v=tdZSrF03-jk
http://www.youtube.com/watch?v=KihQ0rJJXAI

Practice singing the song prior to the children beginning the activity:

> Jesus loves me! This I know,
> for the Bible tells me so.
> Little ones to him belong;
> they are weak, but he is strong.
> Refrain:
> Yes, Jesus loves me! Yes, Jesus loves me!
> Yes, Jesus loves me! The Bible tells me so.
>
> Jesus loves me! This I know,
> as he loved so long ago,
> taking children on his knee,
> saying, "Let them come to me."
> (Refrain)
>
> Jesus loves me still today,
> walking with me on my way,
> wanting as a friend to give
> light and love to all who live.
> (Refrain)

Gather the children in your story/worship area. If you were able to locate pictures of Jesus and children, show them to the children.

Open the Bible and read Hebrews 13: 8. Have them repeat the verse after you several times. Ask if any of them know the song "Jesus Loves Me." If some do, invite them to sing it for the rest of the group. Teach the second and third verses. Get up and dance in a circle as you sing. At the end raise your arms and shout "Jesus, because you love us we can love others!"

5. Paying Taxes Game

To begin, talk with the children about what taxes are and why we pay them. Explain that in Bible times the people in charge were from the city of Rome and were called Romans. The Romans expected everyone to pay taxes to the leader of Rome. Zacchaeus worked for the Romans as a tax collector. In order for him to make money, he would charge people more than the Romans were asking so that he could keep some for himself.

Choose two children to be workers, one to be Zacchaeus, and one to a Roman leader. If there are not enough learners to distribute the roles then write the extra names on pieces of paper and place around the room as pretend players.

Give each worker 25 "coins" (you can use clothespins, beanbags, pennies, plastic coins, and so forth.) and have them stand 10 steps back from a bucket or deep bowl. Give them 30 seconds to toss as many coins, one at a time, into the bucket as they can. If they have time, they can pick up any coins that missed and try again. (You might put a blanket under the bucket or bowl to keep coins from rolling everywhere.)

Explain to the children that this is the money they have earned. Have Zacchaeus count the coins in each bucket and keep three coins for every ten. Zacchaeus now gives 2 coins to the Roman leader and keeps one for himself. Record how much money each worker, Zacchaeus, and the Roman leader have. Continue until every child has had a chance to be a "worker." At the end of the activity, ask the following questions:

* Who ended up with the most money?
* How did you feel about having to pay taxes?
* What if they knew the money would go for something to help them?

6. God's Peaceful Kingdom

To prepare for this activity, locate a copy of the poster *The*

Peaceable Kingdom by John August Swanson and spend time reflecting on it. Use the following questions to guide you in your reflection:

* Which living creatures are depicted?
* Which are missing? Maybe insects are missing? What else?

Gather the children around the poster so that each child can see and is comfortable. Tell them that it might seem like a long time, but you want them to spend one full minute looking at the picture. After the minute is up ask them what they think the picture is about. Allow for all answers and then let them know that this is one man's idea of what God's kingdom will be like when all of creation gets along.

* Ask them who they think the person in the middle is. Allow for all answers.
* Then ask them to pretend that they are the person standing in the middle of all of the animals. How does that make them feel?
* Ask them why they think there is a peacock in the middle along with the person. Again allow for all answers.
* Then let them know that the peacock's tail with its "eye" reminded the early Christians of how God is able to see all things.
* Let the children pick out different animals to act out.
* Have them show what it is like when the animals don't get along and then what it will be like when God's Kingdom is realized and all live in peace.

Sending and Serving

7. "Please and Thank You" Circle
Gather the children around a table. Explain that each of them is

going to draw a picture of the group, but first you are going to play a silly game to help them to remember to say "please" and "thank you." They must wait to draw until everyone has a crayon. Remind them that using words like "please" and "thank you" and waiting until everyone has something is part of making others feel welcome.

Give everyone a piece of paper, but hold the container of crayons and stand behind one of the children. Ask the child to the left what color crayon they want. Then have them say to the child on their left "I would like a (color) crayon, please." This request is passed around the circle until it comes to the child you are standing behind, who then asks you. When you give them the crayon, that child says "Thank you" and hands it to the child to the right, who repeats "thank you." The crayon continues around the circle until it reaches the child who originally asked. You now ask the child to the left of the first one.

Hint: You can remain standing behind the first child, which means that each request/thank you cycle gets shorter or you can move one child to the left each time so that it remains the same. Which method you choose will depend on the age level and number of children that you have. Once everyone has their first crayon, make the rest available as you normally would and allow them to draw a picture of the group.

8. Greetings in Other Languages
Prior to the lesson, perform an online search to find out how different cultures say hello. Here are some possibilities:

http://www.youtube.com/watch?v=c-2gktk55bI
http://www.youtube.com/watch?v=NmpNE0HR7mg
http://www.youtube.com/watch?v=Hv1TCB3Zoio

Practice saying hello as you will be teaching the children the greetings. Write each greeting with its pronunciation and country of origin on separate pieces of paper. Post each one in different areas around the room along with pictures of people from the different countries.

Gather the children around the globe or world map and invite them to go on a trip around the world with you. Using the globe or map, show the children the places you will visit. Walk (or "fly") to your first stop, practice the greeting and look at the pictures. Explain that not every culture uses a handshake when greeting others. Talk about and practice the forms of greeting that are appropriate for the countries you have chosen. Continue around the room in this way. When you return to your gathering area place a dot sticker on the globe or map showing the countries you "visited."

9. Blessings

As the leader, consider some of the ways that you have been blessed. Think about the children in your group and how they have been a blessing to you. Create a "Blessing Bowl" for the activity, which is simply a bowl with a small amount of water. You will also need roll-on glitter scents, baby oil, or olive oil.

Gather the children in a circle. Explain: a blessing is something good and can also be a prayer. Ask them to name some things that they think are blessings. Allow for all answers and be prepared to share some ideas of your own. Tell them that you are going to close your time together with a special blessing.

Show them the Blessing Bowl and explain that you will make the sign of the cross on the back of their hand using the water, roll-on glitter, or oil. As you go around the circle say "(child's name) God be with you this week" while you dip your finger in the water and make the sign of the cross. Once they understand what you are doing, the children can also pass the blessing around the circle, but you may want to hold on to the bowl of water or oil.

When everyone has been blessed (including you), hold hands

and say a short prayer thanking God for your time together. You may want to end each session together in this way.

Reflect

Take a few minutes to think about the time you have spent with the children as you did these activities.

- * What have you learned about the group?
- * How did they show hospitality to one another?
- * How did you show hospitality to them?
- * Where was God present in your time together?

2

Scripture

Bible Focus Passages

Genesis 18:1-15

The Lord appeared to Abraham by the oaks of Mamre, as he sat at the entrance of his tent in the heat of the day. He looked up and saw three men standing near him. When he saw them, he ran from the tent entrance to meet them, and bowed down to the ground. He said, "My lord, if I find favor with you, do not pass by your servant. Let a little water be brought, and wash your feet, and rest yourselves under the tree. Let me bring a little bread, that you may refresh yourselves, and after that you may pass on—since you have come to your servant." So they said, "Do as you have said." And Abraham hastened into the tent to Sarah, and said, "Make ready quickly three measures of choice flour, knead it, and make cakes." Abraham ran to the herd, and took a calf, tender and good, and gave it to the servant, who hastened to prepare it. Then he took curds and milk and the calf that he had prepared, and set it before them; and he stood by them under the tree while they ate.

They said to him, "Where is your wife Sarah?" And he said, "There, in the tent." Then one said, "I will surely return to you in due season, and your wife Sarah shall have a son." And Sarah was listening at the tent entrance behind him. Now Abraham and Sarah were old, advanced in age; it had ceased to be with Sarah after the manner of women. So Sarah laughed to herself, saying, "After I have grown old, and my husband is old, shall I have pleasure?" The Lord said to Abraham, "Why did Sarah laugh, and say, 'Shall I indeed bear a child, now that I am old?' Is anything too wonderful for the Lord? At the set time I will return to you, in due season, and Sarah shall have a son." But Sarah denied, saying, "I did not laugh"; for she was afraid. He said, "Oh yes, you did laugh."

Genesis 21:1-17
The Lord dealt with Sarah as he had said, and the Lord did for Sarah as he had promised. Sarah conceived and bore Abraham a son in his old age, at the time of which God had spoken to him. Abraham gave the name Isaac to his son whom Sarah bore him. And Abraham circumcised his son Isaac when he was eight days old, as God had commanded him. Abraham was a hundred years old when his son Isaac was born to him. Now Sarah said, "God has brought laughter for me; everyone who hears will laugh with me." And she said, "Who would ever have said to Abraham that Sarah would nurse children? Yet I have borne him a son in his old age." The child grew, and was weaned; and Abraham made a great feast on the day that Isaac was weaned.

But Sarah saw the son of Hagar the Egyptian, whom she had borne to Abraham, playing with her son Isaac. So she said to Abraham, "Cast out this slave woman with her son; for the son of this slave woman shall not inherit along with my son Isaac." The matter was very distressing to Abraham on account of his son. But God said to Abraham, "Do not be distressed because of the boy and because of your slave woman; whatever Sarah says to you, do as she tells you, for it is through Isaac that offspring shall be named for you. As for the son of the slave woman, I will make a nation of him also, because he is your offspring."

So Abraham rose early in the morning, and took bread and a skin of water, and gave it to Hagar, putting it on her shoulder, along with the child, and sent her away. And she departed, and wandered about in the wilderness of Beer-sheba. When the water in the skin was gone, she cast the child under one of the bushes. Then she went and sat down opposite him a good way off, about the distance of a bowshot; for she said, "Do not let me look on the death of the child." And as she sat opposite him, she lifted up her voice and wept. And God heard the voice of the boy; and the angel of God called to Hagar from heaven, and said to her, "What troubles you, Hagar? Do not be afraid; for God has heard the voice of the boy where he is.

Isaiah 25:1-9

O Lord, you are my God; I will exalt you, I will praise your name; for you have done wonderful things, plans formed of old, faithful and sure. For you have made the city a heap, the fortified city a ruin; the palace of aliens is a city no more, it will never be rebuilt. Therefore strong peoples will glorify you; cities of ruthless nations will fear you. For you have been a refuge to the poor, a refuge to the needy in their distress, a shelter from the rainstorm and a shade from the heat. When the blast of the ruthless was like a winter rainstorm, the noise of aliens like heat in a dry place, you subdued the heat with the shade of clouds; the song of the ruthless was stilled.

On this mountain the Lord of hosts will make for all peoples a feast of rich food, a feast of well-aged wines, of rich food filled with marrow, of well-aged wines strained clear. And he will destroy on this mountain the shroud that is cast over all peoples, the sheet that is spread over all nations; he will swallow up death forever. Then the Lord God will wipe away the tears from all faces, and the disgrace of his people he will take away from all the earth, for the Lord has spoken.

It will be said on that day, Lo, this is our God; we have waited for him, so that he might save us. This is the Lord for whom we have waited; let us be glad and rejoice in his salvation.

About This Exploration

As hospitality and scripture intersect, we acknowledge the many ways people enter and encounter sacred story. Multiple intelligences, cultural experiences, social locations, and life experiences impact the reading and interpretation of scripture. This invites dialogue, mutual learning, and broadened understanding. Hospitality requires a commitment to multiple expressions of the story. We honor one another and one another's viewpoints. We are called to embody scripture in the context of a diverse world with many sacred texts. At the intersection of hospitality and scripture, the sacred story challenges and changes all.

Young children can anticipate the arrival of special guests. They enjoy preparing for others to visit. Just as Abraham stood ready to invite in any one who came by, children are usually ready to have someone come over to play. However, they are not nearly as concerned as adults are about the neatness of the house or the presentation of the food. They also enjoy preparing to visit others, such going to see their grandparents or other relatives, when they know that they are loved unconditionally and will be welcomed.

Description of Bible Focus Passages
Does the arrival of visitors spur a cleaning spree at your house? As you read the Genesis text notice the biblical example of Abraham and Sarah who, at a moment's notice, are prepared to entertain visitors. Being able to extend hospitality to others has far more to do with one's attitude than it does with the actual physical surroundings. Abraham wasn't concerned with shaking out the rugs and plumping the cushions. His primary concern was to offer ways for the visitors to refresh and renew themselves. The prophet Isaiah reminds us that God is our refuge and shelter, a place where we can be refreshed and renewed.

The Isaiah passage is infused with the kind of celebration that Sarah felt at the birth of Isaac and the fulfillment of God's promises to her—joy and celebration and gratitude. However, the context is different. Here, the joy comes not in the form of a beginning but in the form of an end, specifically, the end of oppression. The people of God have experienced hospitality in the form of freedom and relief. This relief and the abundance of blessings (symbolized by a bountiful banquet) will be available for all people.

Prayer
Creator God, thank you for the love and generosity that you show toward me. Help me to be loving and generous with the children who are entrusted to my care. Amen.

Deep and Wide
This book is aimed at persons who are working with younger children ages 3-7. As you prepare for this session, pray for the children who will be in your group and for yourself. Prepare your space to make it welcoming to young children. Include a worship/story area with either a carpet or rug to sit on, or cushions and pillows, or small chairs designed for young children.

The Practices
You may want to scan the list of practices before choosing one. Doing all three activities in a group could take 90-120 minutes. Remember that young children will not be able to focus on an activity for very long. Plan more activities than you think you might need. You can always use your plan later.

Exploring and Engaging

1. Abraham Welcomes Visitors
For this activity you will need to gather a Bible (the NIV translation is a little easier for young children to understand) along with biblical costumes, if available. If you do not have costumes at your disposal, then a simple men's shirts and strips of cloth to

tie around the waist and head will suffice. You should also read Genesis 18:1-15 prior to the children's arrival and think about what you do to make others welcome in your home.

To begin, have each child dress up in a costume. Ask the children what they do at home to get ready for someone who comes to visit them. Tell them that in Bible times people had to walk long distances to go from one town to another. There weren't any hotels or restaurants or roadside rest areas. Also explain that people living in the desert may go for long periods of time without seeing other people, so they were always glad to have visitors and were eager to make them comfortable.

Read the story of Abraham's visitors. As you tell the story again, have the children act it out. You may need to repeat the story several times to give everyone a chance to have the part of Abraham or Sarah or the visitors. Perhaps after the first time, one of the older children will be able to tell the story as the others act it out.

2. Camping Out

To prepare for this activity, read Isaiah 25:1-9 with special attention to verses 4, 6, and 8b and think about your experiences with different types of weather. When have you been caught in a storm either physical or mental? Where did you take refuge?

If the weather allows, set up a simple shelter outside with a small pop-up tent or sheet, table, chairs, and so forth. Gather the children outside of the shelter. Talk about how in biblical times many people lived in tents. Ask if any of them have been camping or spent the night in a tent in their backyard. Ask about the weather and if they were too hot or cold, or if they got wet. Read Isaiah 25:4, 6, and 8b, explaining that this is how a man named Isaiah described God.

If there are enough children, divide the children into two groups, having one group be the "campers," and the other group be the "storm." Have the "storm" move off a ways while the "campers" pretend to set up camp. Let the "storm" start making noise by banging pans and spoons together and spraying water. Have them move closer to the "campers." Ask the "campers" what they should do and encourage them to get into the shelter. After the "storm" passes, trade roles and repeat.

If you do not have enough children to split into groups, then simply act out each element of the story one at a time. To end, gather in your shelter for a snack. Offer a prayer of thanksgiving for shelter from storms and for the food.

3. A Song of Rejoicing

Other books in this series introduce the hymn "Enter, Rejoice, and Come In" (tune ENTER, REJOICE). For your age group, an alternative is recommended: "This Is the Day." For helps with the music, consider the following renditions:

> http://www.youtube.com/watch?v=ukNYJmKuHuM
> http://www.youtube.com/watch?v=o-lyIldA878
> http://www.youtube.com/watch?v=bPEny6Hwx2E
> http://www.youtube.com/watch?v=8KvYQKNXiWw
> http://www.youtube.com/watch?v=dWYHAksllbg

Remember, this is a fun song so parade in a circle, wave arms and hands, and have a fun time together. You are not seeking perfection, but a sense of joy that each child has come today.

Gather the children in a circle in an area where they will have room to move around. Practice saying "Good Morning" and shaking hands. Tell the children that they are going to learn a song. Introduce it before hearing or singing it. Teach the song one verse at a time by singing it for the children and then having them repeat phrases after you. Have the children stand in a circle with arms outstretched and fingertips touching.

One fund idea is to prepare waving ribbons to help the children express themselves in song. To make the waving ribbons, use 3" wooden or metal hoops and 5' lengths of ribbon, fabric strips, or crepe paper in different colors and widths. Fold the ribbon in half, loop through the hoop, and pull the loose ends through the ribbon loop. Use 3 to 4 ribbons per hoop. Alternatively, the children could just wave shorter lengths of ribbon, but the hoops are fun to have on hand.

Another idea is to pass out the rhythm instruments. Now sing while playing and moving along. You can move around the circle, in and out of the circle, even have a parade through the house. If you use rhythm instruments, let the children trade them around so each gets a turn with as many as possible (or as they want).

Discerning and Deciding

4. Root of Hospitality

To prepare for this activity, look up meanings for hospitality and related words. Using a different color marker for each word, make a list in a column on newsprint of these words: hospitality, hospital, hospice, hostel, hostess, and host. Post the list in the room at the children's eye level. While most young children cannot yet read, some are beginning to recognize and name letters.

Gather the children around the posted list. Ask them what they notice about all of the words (they all start with the same 3 letters). Read the words, and after each word ask the children if they know what that word means. Explain "hospitality" and see if they can work out the meanings of the next few words.

Some children may have experience with a family member being under hospice care. Explain that a hospice is a place where you can be taken care of, and that there are special types of hotels called hospices so that they don't associate the word just with death.

Talk about host and hostess. Explain that they are the host or hostess whenever someone comes to visit them at their home. Review all the words and ask the children again what they all have in common. If they don't name it, point out that along with the similar spellings, they all have to do with taking care of others or providing a safe place for others.

5. What Would You Want?

For this activity you will need to locate some pictures of Bible lands, both ancient and modern. To help you in your search, many Bibles and Bible reference books include photos. You can also check your church library or the Internet (www.bibleplaces.com) to build your picture gallery.

Gather the children and show them the pictures of Bible lands starting with those from ancient times. Explain that this is the area where the people we read about in the Bible lived, the place where Jesus grew up and did his ministry. Study the pictures with the children and collectively think about what it would be like to have lived during Bible times. Use the following questions for discussion:

* How might living in that same geographic area be different now?
* If you lived there, what kinds of things would you want or need?

Working through each set of pictures, have the children brainstorm items they would need if they lived in that land. Some examples are: water, nuts, tent, camel, and so forth. There are no right answers here, but you can point out why one might be better than another in the desert.

Give each child a piece of paper and ask them to draw a picture on the back where they pretend they are living in Bible lands and are inviting someone into their home. If there is time, look at the more modern pictures and talk about how they are similar yet different.

6. Sandy Painting

For this activity, you will need finger paint. If you do not have pre-mixed finger paint available, you can make finger paint by combining 1 cup of powdered laundry detergent with 3 tablespoons of liquid tempera and ¼ cup of water (or mixing ¼ cup of liquid starch with powdered paint). Whether you make your own paint or buy pre-mixed finger paint, add just enough sand to the paint to give the paint a grainy texture.

Be forewarned that young children and finger paint can create a mess so make sure you choose an appropriate space! If you add a few drops of liquid soap to the paint and blend this will help to make cleanup easier, especially if the paint gets on clothes. Ideal is to provide a smock or apron for each child. (Discarded, but freshly laundered men's shirts work well as smocks.)

To begin the activity, remind the children that the land of the Bible stories is dry and dusty. Invite them to make a sandy painting of a desert. Encourage the children to finger paint a picture, but have the brushes ready if they don't like that sensory experience. As the children finish, set aside their paintings to dry. Provide a tub of water for them to wash their hands.

Sending and Serving

7. Abraham, Abraham, Visitor

This activity includes a modified version of the classic children's game "Duck, Duck, Goose" only for this purpose the game will become "Abraham, Abraham, Visitor." If you do not have enough young learners to play a game of "Abraham, Abraham, Visitor" then you can simply act out the scene that happens at the end of each round.

Gather the children outside or in an area where you will have some room to move. Choose one child to be Abraham (or Sarah), and have the rest sit in a circle. "Abraham" goes around the circle, tapping children on the shoulder and calling each "Abraham" until he or she picks one to be the "Visitor."

The "visitor" stands and the two children run (or walk fast) around the circle in opposite directions. When they meet, they must high five each other. The first child returns to the empty spot, stops, bows to the other child and says, "welcome to my tent." The child who was "Abraham" will now sit down and the other child becomes the new "Abraham." Continue playing until everyone who wants to has a chance to be Abraham. Let the children decide if they would rather be "Abraham" or "Sarah," and use that name as they go around the circle.

8. Something for Others

This activity will require some preparation as you will need to speak with whoever runs your church nursery. Ask them if there is a toy or book that they need or what snacks they keep on hand for the children. From the list of suggestions, purchase a few needed items. You will also need newspaper, coffee filters and markers.

Gather the children and show them what you have brought for the children in the nursery. Explain whom this gift is for and how the gift might be used. Tell them that you are also going to make some decorations for those children.

Spread newspapers on the table and floor. Have the children put on smocks, aprons or old men's shirts. Help the children fold the coffee filters into quarters. Then lightly spray both sides with water to dampen. To decorate the filters, the children will hold markers of different colors against the dampened coffee filter so that the color has a chance to bleed into the damp areas. They may want to work from both sides. Open the filters and set aside to dry. (You may want to use a hair dryer to speed the process.)

As they work, give the children the opportunity to talk about how they feel about giving something to someone else and not being able to have something for themselves. Ask some wonder questions such as:

* "I wonder how the children in the nursery will feel about our gifts?"
* "I wonder how you feel about giving a gift."
* "I wonder how you feel about getting gifts."

Visit the nursery and deliver the gifts and decorations.

9. Greeting Others

For this activity you will need to research greetings used in other cultures (see also activity 8, chapter 1, if you didn't do that activity). By using a simple online search engine you should be able to find various articles or videos regarding cultural greetings.

To begin, ask the learners to think about all of the ways that you have seen others extend greetings (handshake, high five, hug, kiss, pat on the back, sports team hand slaps, and so forth). Next, read Genesis 18:1-5 with the children. You may choose to simply read straight from the text or use storytelling to talk about the event. Ask the following questions:

* How did Abraham greet his guests?
* How do you greet others?

Talk about different ways you say hello to people. Be sure to include some from the list and websites above. Then ask the children about the ways they say goodbye to someone.

* Are farewells the same as greetings?
* Divide the children into pairs and practice saying hello and goodbye in different ways.

As the children leave today, say to each one, "God loves you, and so do I." Maybe you will want to bless them in this way every week.

Reflect

* In what ways are you and the children gaining a new understanding of the meaning of hospitality?
* Is it easier for you to extend hospitality or to receive it from others?
* Where do you see hospitality happening in your everyday life?

3

Discipleship

Bible Focus Passages

John 13:1-17, 31b-35

Now before the festival of the Passover, Jesus knew that his hour had come to depart from this world and go to the Father. Having loved his own who were in the world, he loved them to the end. The devil had already put it into the heart of Judas son of Simon Iscariot to betray him. And during supper Jesus, knowing that the Father had given all things into his hands, and that he had come from God and was going to God, got up from the table, took off his outer robe, and tied a towel around himself. Then he poured water into a basin and began to wash the disciples' feet and to wipe them with the towel that was tied around him. He came to Simon Peter, who said to him, 'Lord, are you going to wash my feet?' Jesus answered, 'You do not know now what I am doing, but later you will understand.' Peter said to him, 'You will never wash my feet.' Jesus answered, 'Unless I wash you, you have no share with me.' Simon Peter said to him, 'Lord, not my feet only but also my hands and my head!' Jesus said to him, 'One who has bathed does not need to wash, except for the feet, but is entirely clean. And you are clean, though not all of you.' For he knew who was to betray him; for this reason he said, 'Not all of you are clean.'

After he had washed their feet, had put on his robe, and had returned to the table, he said to them, 'Do you know what I have done to you? You call me Teacher and Lord—and you are right, for that is what I am. So if I, your Lord and Teacher, have washed your feet, you also ought to wash one another's feet. For I have an example, that you also should do as I have done to you. Very truly, I tell you, servants are not greater than their master, nor are messengers greater than the one who sent them. If you know these things, you are blessed if you do them.

When he had gone out, Jesus said, 'Now the Son of Man has been glorified, and God has been glorified in him. If God has been glorified in him, God will also glorify him in himself and will glorify him at once. Little children, I am with you only a little longer. You will look for me; and as I said to the Jews so now I say to you, "Where I am going, you cannot come." I give you a new commandment, that you love one another. Just as I have loved you, you also should love one another. By this everyone will know that you are my disciples, if you have love for one another.'

Acts 2:42-47

They devoted themselves to the apostles' teaching and fellowship, to the breaking of bread and the prayers.

Awe came upon everyone, because many wonders and signs were being done by the apostles. All who believed were together and had all things in common; they would sell their possessions and goods and distribute the proceeds to all, as any had need. Day by day, as they spent much time together in the temple, they broke bread at home and ate their food with glad and generous hearts, praising God and having the goodwill of all the people. And day by day the Lord added to their number those who were being saved.

About This Exploration

Hospitable disciples see God in each encounter with the people in our daily lives and those who lie beyond our usual circles of experience. The distinctions between other and self decrease when other living creatures and the earth are encountered as a sacred system of interrelationships.

We practice hospitality in cultures with habits of expected interaction. However, Jesus calls us to habits of attentiveness, which go beyond our own cultures, needs, and experiences. As disciples, all can be encouraged to see the face of Jesus in every experience of hospitality.

Hospitality encompasses giving and receiving. Receiving the gift of hospitality from another, even when uncomfortable, embodies receiving God's many gifts to our world.

Reflection on Bible Focus Passages

Being a disciple of Jesus means following him and learning to be more like him in his obedience to God. It is a lifelong process. Helping the children to become disciples of Jesus includes teaching them, but mostly it consists of modeling Christian behavior to the best of your ability.

The John 13 passage is used to remind us that we are to love and serve one another, but we tend to think of the "one another" as those outside of our family circle. Remember that Jesus was washing the feet of his friends, his family, the people he was in contact with daily. The giving and receiving of hospitality should not be limited to "others," but must extend to those we see regularly. How do you extend hospitality to your family? How do you accept hospitality from them? How does this extend to your church family?

Prayer

Generous God, you sent Jesus as an example of your great love and how we should live. Help me to be an example of love and hospitality to these young children. Amen.

Deep and Wide

This book is aimed at persons who are working with younger children ages 3-7. As you prepare for this session, pray for the children who will be in your group and for yourself. Prepare your space to make it welcoming to young children. Include a worship/story area with either a carpet or rug to sit on, or cushions and pillows, or small chairs designed for young children.

Hospitable disciples see God in each encounter with the people in our daily lives and those who lie beyond our usual circles of experience. The distinctions between other and self decrease when other living creatures and the earth are encountered as a sacred system of interrelationships.

We practice hospitality in cultures with habits of expected interaction. However, Jesus calls us to habits of attentiveness, which go beyond our own cultures, needs, and experiences. As disciples, all can be encouraged to see the face of Jesus in every experience of hospitality.

The Practices

You may want to scan the list of practices before choosing one. Doing all three activities in a group could take 90-120 minutes. Remember that young children will not be able to focus on an activity for very long. Plan more activities than you think you might need. You can always use your plan later.

Children learn by example. The Bible stories are important, but it will be how the adults in their lives model the example of Jesus that will have the most effect on them. It is not easy for them to put others first or to think in terms of what is best for the group, but with guidance, practice, and the example of others they will get there.

Exploring and Engaging

1. Following Jesus

To help the children follow the example that Jesus set, this activity involves playing a game of "Jesus Says," similar to the classic children's game "Simon Says."

Ask the children to tell you what the word "disciple" means. Allow for and affirm all responses. Explain to the children that a disciple is someone who follows a leader or teacher and learns from them. Spend some time explaining that there are twelve special disciples listed in the Bible. Ask the children if they can name a disciple (Peter, Andrew, James son of Zebedee, John, Philip, Bartholomew, Matthew, Thomas, James, Thaddaeus, Simon, and Judas). Let the children know that each of us is a disciple, too. Ask them why would God call us disciples and allow for responses. Let the children know that we are called disciples because we want to follow and learn from Jesus just like the original disciples did.

Next, play the game "Jesus Says" with the children. The leader should be the first to have Jesus say to do things like give a hug, shake hands, dance for joy, shout "Amen," along with the usual fun actions. If someone follows the directions that don't begin with "Jesus says," say "Jesus says to try again." Since the group isn't reduced when they misstep, you will need to pick a new leader every few commands and continue the game until all the children have had a chance to be Jesus.

2. Dusty Road Footprints and Foot Washing

To prepare yourself for this activity make sure you have read the story of Jesus washing the disciples' feet in John 13:1-17 and 31-35. Then gather the following supplies for this activity as the children will be making "dusty" footprints and experiencing a mini foot washing:

* Bible
* Pair of sandals
* Large drop cloth or plastic tablecloths
* Two strips of white butcher paper or other heavy paper each about 4' long
* Liquid tempera paint in several colors

* Dish washing liquid
* Pie tins or other shallow dishes to hold the paint
* Chairs
* Towels
* Several small tubs of water

Gather the children and read the scripture passage to them. Explain to them that in Bible times people wore sandals or went barefoot. Most of them walked everywhere they went, and the roads were very dusty. Look at the pair of sandals and talk about how dirty your feet would get. Tell them that a good host would always have water and towels ready to wash the feet of guests so that they would feel clean and refreshed.

Let them know that you are going to make "dusty road" footprints and help one another by washing their feet. Spread out the drop cloth and lay the strips of paper on top of it, place the pie tins with a small amount of paint in them at one end and the chairs, basins of water, and towels at the other end. Station one child at the foot-washing end of each strip. Have the other children line up at the paint end and remove their shoes and socks.

One at a time let the children pick two colors of paint and step into it. Then, with paint on their feet, they will walk down the strip to the other end of the paper and sit in the chair. Have them wait until you are available to wash their feet.

Assure the children that it is okay if the footprints overlap since that is what would happen on the road. You may want to turn you paper around half way through so that you have footprints going in both directions. Don't forget walk down the road as well and let a child wash your feet.

3. Ways of Serving Others

Perform an online image search for the painting *The Barber Shop* by Jacob Lawrence. Before you work with the children, spend some time looking at the image. Consider the following questions:

* What are these men doing for each other?
* Who exactly is serving and who is being served?
* What kind of conversation might be going on?

Reflect on the time you have spent in a barbershop or beauty parlor. To finish your personal meditation, read John 13:1-17, 31-35 and brainstorm ways that the children in your group might serve others.

Gather the children around the computer screen where all can see and sit comfortably. Tell them that you are going to spend one minute just sitting and looking at the poster. Now ask them what they think is going on in the picture. Allow for all answers, and then explain that it is a barbershop. Ask them about their experiences getting their hair cut. Use the following questions as a discussion guide:

* Where do they go?
* Who does it?
* Do they get their hair washed?
* Is it easy to sit still?

Explain that the people who cut our hair are doing us a service. They are helping us with something that we need to have done.

Remind the children that Jesus served others. Ask if they can think of any way that Jesus did things for others. Share or review the John 13:1-17 "Washing Feet" story with them. Ask:

* What are some things that need to be done around our room?
* What are some tasks that we could do?
* What are some things they could do at home to serve

others? (put away dishes, take out the trash, give a hug, dust)

Using the card stock quarters have them make coupons that they can give to their parents or other family members listing something that they can do. Before you end your time together, remind them of the things that they said they could do in your room and get them done! Lead the children in a short prayer thanking God for the people who help us and for our ability to help others.

Discerning and Deciding

4. Servant Song
Search online to find the hymn by Richard Gillard, "Won't You Let Me Be Your Servant." (It's also in *New Century Hymnal*, hymn 539). Note: The hymn was inspired by Mark 9:35 where Jesus says to the disciples, "Whoever wants to be first must be last of all and servant of all." Review the words and music to the hymn and spend some time thinking about what it means to you. Hint: If you are not familiar with the hymn, ask someone from your choir or your music leader to help you learn this hymn so that you can teach it to the children. Decide how many verses your group can easily learn. Plan on at least the first two:

Gather the children together and remind them that you have been talking about serving others and showing hospitality. Tell them that they are going to learn a new song about serving others. Sing the song for them one time. In addition to singing, it might be helpful to create actions to go along with the words. You can either use your own or follow the suggested actions at the end of the activity. Then start teaching it to them, along with the actions, one line at a time.

Agony: point index fingers at each other and jab together

twice

Christ (Jesus)- with middle finger of right hand touch palm of left hand, then reverse.

Find harmony/all we've known: link arms

Hear: point to ear

Heaven: point to sky

I/me/my: point to self

Journey through: walk in place

Joy: look joyful

Laugh: point to your big smile

Love: cross arms at wrists over chest

Peace: hands out in front of you, palms down

Pray: hands together in prayer

Servant: palms up in front of you move hands back and forth, then palms facing and shoulder height move down to waist height.

Sing: hand to side of mouth

Sorrow: look sad

Speak: point to mouth

Weep: point to eyes and move fingers down cheeks

You: point to other person

5. All for One and One for All Picnic

In the early church, the followers pooled their resources to make the best use of them and to be able to take care of others (see, for example, Acts 2:42-47, 4:32-37). To demonstrate this, you will be hosting a picnic for the children, preferably outside if weather permits. To prepare, gather one grocery bag for each child. Place one item you will need for the picnic in each bag, leaving one bag empty. Tape or tie shut each bag. (Suggested items include: crackers, cookies, juice, cups, napkins, blanket, and so forth.)

Have the children sit in a circle and place one bag behind each of them. Be sure to use the empty bag as well as those essential for your picnic. Ask the children, "What are some things that you might need for a picnic?" Allow for responses. Next, have them open the bag behind them. As they are opening their bags ask, "Can you have a picnic with just a ____?" and fill in the blank with their item. Continue this for each learner. Read Acts 2:42-47, highlighting how everyone put their belongings together for all to use. Announce that that is what you are doing for your picnic. Hopefully the children will agree with that idea. Follow through with it and enjoy your picnic.

6. Alike and Different

Read Acts 2:42-47. Think about the children in your group and how they are alike and how they are different from one another. Remember that the disciples traveled to other countries and other cultures sharing the word of God with all. Before you start the activity, write the following headings on blank paper: Color, Food, Animal, Game/Toy, Movie/TV Show, Book. Tape these pages in different areas of your room. Then, gather a globe and locate Israel, Greece, and Italy.

As the children arrive, take them around to the different interest papers and ask them for their favorite color, food, and so forth., writing their response on the paper. After everyone has had a chance to respond, collect the papers and gather the children in a circle. Show them the paper headed Color and read all the different colors that are listed. Point out when the same color is listed more than once. Ask the children:

* Should we treat someone differently just because they like a different color than we do?
* Should we be nicer to someone who likes the same color as we do?
* Continue through all the papers in a similar manner.

Tell the children that the first disciples went to other countries to share God's word and the teachings of Jesus. Show them Israel,

Greece, and Italy on the globe. Ask them if they think that the people in all these countries looked the same, dressed the same, and liked the same food. If they answer yes, let them know that while there may have been some things that were similar, there were many things that were different just like in your group.

Tell them that Jesus came to help us learn to share God's love with everyone even if they are different from us. Read or review Acts 2: 42-47. Ask them if they think God wants us to treat people differently just because they may have a different skin color, different clothing, or like different foods. Remind them that God loves all of us equally. Encourage them to think of things that they can do for others. Lead the children in a brief prayer thanking God for all the ways that we are different.

Sending and Serving

7. Welcome to Our Room

For this activity, spend some time thinking about preparing your home for visitors. Are there areas that are always ready and others that require major cleaning? Do you prepare differently for friends coming over for the evening versus someone coming to spend the weekend?

Read Acts 2: 42-46. The early followers met in one another's homes on a regular basis, sharing food, fellowship, learning, and prayers. Then before this activity starts, gather some cleaning supplies (see below).

Gather the children in your story/worship area and ask them:

* What do you do to get ready for company?
* How do you help your parents prepare for guests?

What do you do for guests when they arrive?

* Think about your room. What are some things that you

would need to do (or have help with) before someone could be invited in?

Now, let's get to work in your meeting room! Wipe off tables and chairs with damp sponges or rags. (You might want to be the one who rinses and wrings them out.) Push in chairs, pick up toys, sweep the floor. Invite older siblings and parents to wait at the door of the "house". Have the children line up at the door and say "Welcome to our room!" as you open it. Let the children show them around your newly cleaned room. Stand at the door and, as each person leaves say, "Thank you for coming today." Give them a hug, handshake, or gentle pat on the shoulder.

8. Fellowship Time
For this activity you will be inviting friends or siblings of the children to come over as guests for a fellowship time that the learners will prepare. Make sure that arrangements have been ahead of time for the guests to come. The guests should arrive approximately a half hour to forty-five minutes later than the learners.

Gather the children around a table and talk about what fellowship means. Ask them to consider how they experience fellowship in the group. Explain that you are going to make trail mix and decorate a table covering to be used for when the guests arrive. Begin by having everyone clean their hands. Also remind the children that if they have to cough or sneeze, they should step away from the table. Assure them that they will get to eat some of the treat later and that they should not eat any while they are fixing it.

Set out the ingredients (nuts, raisins, pretzels, chocolate pieces, corn square cereal, and so forth.) and let the children take turns adding scoops of each one to a large bowl. Take turns stirring the mixture as items are added. When this is done, cover the bowl with plastic wrap and set aside. Now spread out paper over the table and let the children decorate it.

By this time the guests should have arrived and be ready to come to fellowship time. Allow the children to serve the guests first before they begin enjoying the snack. When the time is ended, thank them for their hospitality.

9. "Be Church" Game

Gather the children in an area where they can move around. Share the Bible story about the early church from Acts 2:42-47. Help them to describe some of the things the early Christians did together such as praying, eating, breaking bread, praising God, learning, and so forth.

Depending on the ages of your children, choose 4 to 6 of these activities and come up with a simple action for each one. (See activity 4 in this chapter for a list of song actions that may give you ideas as well.) List them on a piece of paper. Practice these actions a couple of times.

Tell the children that you going to play a "Be Church" game. Have them scatter through the area you are using. When the leader calls out "be church" they should run around the area until the leader calls out one of the words on your list. Then they will stop where they are and do the action until the leader calls "be church" again. Continue in this manner mixing up the actions. You may want to let the children take turns being the leader.

Close by ending with a prayer or praising God action and have everyone sit where they are while you lead them in a brief prayer thanking God for the first Christians, your church, and the fun you have had.

Reflect

* In what ways are the children thinking about others more?
* In what ways are they pleased about participating in the

life of the church?
* In what ways are they learning to become disciples, followers, of Jesus?

It may feel like a one step forward, two steps backward process, but it is the same for adults. The fact that you care enough to spend time with them is more important than you know. You are both blessed and a blessing. See if you can make a list of all the ways that is true.

4

Christian Tradition

Bible Focus Passages

Mark 14:22-25
While they were eating, he took a loaf of bread, and after blessing it he broke it, gave it to them, and said, "Take; this is my body." Then he took a cup, and after giving thanks he gave it to them, and all of them drank from it. He said to them, "This is my blood of the covenant, which is poured out for many. Truly I tell you, I will never again drink of the fruit of the vine until that day when I drink it new in the kingdom of God."

1 Corinthians 11:23-36
For I received from the Lord what I also handed on to you, that the Lord Jesus on the night when he was betrayed took a loaf of bread, and when he had given thanks, he broke it and said, "This is my body that is for you. Do this in remembrance of me." In the same way he took the cup also, after supper, saying, "This cup is the new covenant in my blood. Do this, as often as you drink it, in remembrance of me." For as often as you eat this bread and drink the cup, you proclaim the Lord's death until he comes. Whoever, therefore, eats the bread or drinks the cup of the Lord in an unworthy manner will be answerable for the body and blood of the Lord. Examine yourselves, and only then eat of the bread and drink of the cup. For all who eat and drink without discerning the body, eat and drink judgment against themselves. For this reason many of you are weak and ill, and some have died. But if we judged ourselves, we would not be judged. But when we are judged by the Lord, we are disciplined so that we

may not be condemned along with the world. So then, my brothers and sisters, when you come together to eat, wait for one another. If you are hungry, eat at home, so that when you come together, it will not be for your condemnation. About the other things I will give instructions when I come.

1 Peter 4:1-11

Since therefore Christ suffered in the flesh, arm yourselves also with the same intention (for whoever has suffered in the flesh has finished with sin), so as to live for the rest of your earthly life no longer by human desires but by the will of God. You have already spent enough time in doing what the Gentiles like to do, living in licentiousness, passions, drunkenness, revels, carousing, and lawless idolatry.

They are surprised that you no longer join them in the same excesses of dissipation, and so they blaspheme. But they will have to give an accounting to him who stands ready to judge the living and the dead. For this is the reason the gospel was proclaimed even to the dead, so that, though they had been judged in the flesh as everyone is judged, they might live in the spirit as God does.

The end of all things is near; therefore be serious and discipline yourselves for the sake of your prayers. Above all, maintain constant love for one another, for love covers a multitude of sins. Be hospitable to one another without complaining. Like good stewards of the manifold grace of God, serve one another with whatever gift each of you has received. Whoever speaks must do so as one speaking the very words of God; whoever serves must do so with the strength that God supplies, so that God may be glorified in all things through Jesus Christ. To him belong the glory and the power forever and ever. Amen.

About This Exploration

God continually invites us to extravagantly welcome others into abundant life. We are not the first to experience questions, failures, accomplishments, joys and sorrows. Our Christian tradition gives us ancestors in faith whose stories and life experiences inform our own. Every drop of water reminds us of Christ's baptism. Shared meals recall Jesus' breaking bread and sharing the cup. Grounded in Hebrew tradition, Jesus displayed radical commitment to the poor. Love for the poor continues to characterize Christian community. God invites us to welcome those whom we encounter in daily life, and those we might not otherwise encounter, to see them as God's beloved people, and treasure the diversity of humanity. We are called by God to create a safe, welcoming environment for all. We join the family of all time.

Description of Bible Focus Passages
Children this age tend to be quite literal, which can make the Mark passage rather scary for them. If it is possible, using "The Last Supper" from *Living God's Way* by Ralph Milton (Kelowna, B.C.: Wood Lake Publishing, n.d.) will be especially helpful for this Exploration. Regardless of which version of the story you use, put more emphasis on the why of communion- that we do this to remember Jesus and to connect us with other Christians. The youngest children in this group are just beginning to get the feel of yearly traditions, but daily and weekly routines are important to them. It is helpful for them if you have an opening and closing ritual that you use each session. They can feel the importance of the ritual routine of Communion long before they will understand it.

Both of the readings about the Last Supper suggest that the sharing of the bread and wine took place after the regular Passover meal. This would indicate that Jesus was adding to, rather than replacing, this observance. The 1Peter passage tells us to be hospitable without complaining and to serve to the best of our God given abilities. Jesus was the prime example of this.

* How do you go about your daily life?
* Are you able to cheerfully extend hospitality to others?
* Do you complete the task at hand to the best of your abilities?

One day, one task at a time, make a conscious effort to not complain and to function to your best. Make a list of all of the jobs/professions that are service oriented. Take time to remember Jesus.

Deep and Wide
This book is aimed at persons who are working with younger children ages 3-7. As you prepare for this session, pray for the children who will be in your group and for yourself. Prepare your space to make it welcoming to young children. Include a worship/story area with either a carpet or rug to sit on, or cushions and pillows, or small chairs designed for young children.

As you prepare for this session, pray for each child who will be in your group and for yourself. Prepare your space so that it will be welcoming to young children. Include a worship/story area. Think about the traditions of your church family and your own family. Do they have similarities? Do they overlap in any way?

Prayer
Creator and Helper of us all, as I work with these children let me give them my best efforts. Let my words and actions be a reflection of your great love for all of us. Amen

The Practices

You may want to scan the list of practices before choosing one. Doing all three activities in a group could take 90-120 minutes. Remember that young children will not be able to focus on an activity for very long. Plan more activities than you think you might need. You can always use your plan later.

Exploring and Engaging

1. Traditions

To prepare for this activity, think about the traditions that your church or family uses to mark its worship time and the year. Are these traditions rooted in the Bible? Some traditions become such a part of our routine that they are hard to change. Other traditions can have a great deal of variation as long as they happen.

Gather the children in your worship or story area. Talk with them about some of the routines they have in their family, such as getting ready for bed at night and getting ready in the morning. Then talk about the way they celebrate their birthday. Tell them that that routine is a tradition, something that their family does every year. Ask them to describe some other traditions in their family such as Christmas or Easter celebrations. Write their ideas on a piece of paper.

Show the children the Bible and tell them that our most important church traditions come from the Bible. Talk about showing hospitality, sharing with others, and taking care of others. Let them know that worshipping, praying and eating together are all things that the Bible tells us we should do. The people who believe in God and Jesus have been doing these things for thousands of years.

Make a list of things that happen in your services of worship each week such as a time of greeting or passing of the peace, lighting of candles, music, prayers, offerings and communion. Give the children a chance to share their favorite traditions from church or home. If there is time, invite them to draw a picture of it.

2. Passing the Peace

To prepare, take some time to think about how your congregation "passes the peace" (or other ritual of welcome or interaction among worshipers).

* It is separate from the time of greeting?
* Do you use special words?
* Is there a story about how your congregation either has passed down this tradition or adopted it?

Locate a copy of the poster *Embrace of Peace* by George Tooker and spend time reflecting on it. If you cannot obtain a hard copy of the poster then a simple online image search should suffice.

Gather the children in your worship/story area. Explain that "passing the peace" is a special way of greeting others and that you are going to practice how to do it. If your congregation has special words that are used during worship then use those. If not, use "Peace be with you," and respond with "And also with you." So that the children will understand this practice, go to each child and say, "Peace be with you," and have the child respond to you, "And also with you."

Then have one child stand in front of the group and say "Peace be with you" and the group respond "And also with you." Give every child a chance to be the leader. If your group is large, divide into pairs so that they can shake hands or give a hug as they extend peace to one another. If it is a small group then simply take turns extending peace to one another.

Show the children the poster *Embrace of Peace* or have it ready on the computer screen where everyone can see. Ask them to spend one minute quietly looking at the picture, and then give them the opportunity to tell what they see. Ask them the following questions to lead them in discussion:

* What are the people doing?
* Where might they be?
* How are they feeling?

Each time your group gathers you might want to include passing the peace as part of your opening time.

3. Bread and Grapes

For this activity you and the children will share a friendship meal together centered on the ancient biblical practice. You will want to share this activity and menu with parents ahead of time so that any dietary concerns can be shared or meal quantities before or afterward can be adjusted.

For the meal itself, gather a variety of breads and crackers (try to include pita bread, flatbread crackers, and soft pretzels along with more traditional breads), several kinds of grapes and water or juice. If you are feeling adventurous, you might include feta cheese, hummus, cucumber, dates, raisins, and honey- typical foods in the Middle East.

Gather the children and have everyone wash their hands. Explain that you are going to have a friendship meal together. Show the children the different foods that you have brought. Ask if this reminds them of a special meal that you have talked about before. Allow for all answers, but steer them toward Jesus' Last Supper and communion. Share the story with them. Have the children help you pass out plates, cups, and napkins while you cut or break the bread in to portion size pieces. Offer a mealtime blessing, or invite one of the children to do this. Depending on the age of the children in your group, you can pass the different breads and grapes around or you may want to serve them yourself. Encourage everyone to try at least a taste of the different types. As you share this meal together ask the children about which foods they do and don't like. This is also a great opportunity to talk about their week and give them a chance to share.

Discerning and Deciding

4. Who Is Coming? Charades

This activity uses a simple game of charades to build anticipation for dinner guests. The charade game pieces should all describe someone who is coming to visit. The following is a list of ideas or you can create your own:

* Older person with a cane or walker
* Blind person
* Mother with a baby
* Butterfly
* Deaf person
* Person on crutches
* Person in a wheelchair
* Person who is sad
* Person who is hungry
* Dog
* Friend

Gather the children in a semicircle. Explain that you are going to play a game of charades where they will each act out someone who might come to visit. Once they guess who it is, they need to come up with ways to make the visitor feel welcome. Then they can act that out as well. Make sure that everyone who desires has a chance to act out someone or something.

Be prepared to give hints to both the actors and the guessers! You may need to allow the youngest children to make noises or speak.

5. "Wade in the Water"

For this activity you will need to familiarize yourself with the song "Wade in the Water". Below suggests incorporating red, blue, and white streamers, so you will need to gather or construct those should that appeal to you. If you are not familiar with the song then a simple Internet search should help you find a free online recording. Below are the lyrics:

> Verse 1:
> Well, who are these children all dressed in red?
> God's a-gonna trouble the water
> Must be the children that Moses led
> God's a-gonna trouble the water.
> Chorus:
> Wade in the water.
> Wade in the water, children.
> Wade in the water.
> God's gonna trouble the water.
> Verse 2:
> Who's that young girl dressed in white?
> Wade in the Water
> Must be the Children of Israelites
> God's gonna trouble the Water.
> (Chorus)
> Jordan's water is chilly and cold.
> God's gonna trouble the water.
> It chills the body, but not the soul.
> God's gonna trouble the water.
> (Chorus)
> If you get there before I do.
> God's gonna trouble the water.
> Tell all of my friends I'm coming too.
> God's gonna trouble the water.
> (Chorus)

Remember that this is to be an enjoyable experience and that you are not seeking perfection from them or you. Make it fun.

Gather the children in a circle in an area where you will have room to move around. Have the children practice saying "Good morning" and shaking hands.

Next, ask the children if they can think of a time when we use water in church. Tell the children the history of the song "Wade in the Water" by explaining that slaves used water as a way to "clean off" their scent so that they could not be followed. Tell them that when someone is baptized water is used as a symbol that God has made them clean.

Start by teaching the children the chorus. Have them side step around the circle, changing direction with each repetition of "wade in the water." Do an all over body shake on "God's gonna trouble the water."

Show the children the Bible and explain that the verses refer to stories in it. Distribute red, white, and blue streamers, telling the children to wave their color when it is mentioned. Sing or say each verse, doing the chorus with motions in between.

6. "Living as Jesus" Game

For this lesson the children will need to use some basic critical thinking skills, as they will be examining statements in relationship to God. Prior to the activity, review the activity description and review the list of statements. Spend time thinking about the little things you do every day. Do they bring you closer to God in some way or do they hold you back?

"Living as Jesus" game statements:

* Praying
* Sharing toys
* Calling someone names
* Taking a walk
* Throwing trash on the ground

- Reading a story to someone
- Carrying a package for someone
- Throwing eggs at someone's house
- Getting a drink for someone
- Giving someone a hug
- Telling someone they are stupid
- Helping someone who is hurt
- Grabbing a toy
- Hitting someone
- Reading the Bible
- Fixing food for someone
- Praising God

Gather the children in an area where they can make a circle. This game can be played outside if the weather permits. Use a rope to make a circle and have the children stand just inside the circle. If you are playing outside, you could draw a circle on pavement with chalk. Stand in the middle of the circle and read 1Peter 4:8 -11.

Place the Bible in the middle and step outside of the circle. Tell the children that you are going to say some different things. They have to decide if it will take them closer to God or if it will take them away from God. If it will take them closer, they are to take one step toward the Bible. If it will take them farther away, they are to take one step back. Mix up the statements and add some of your own, but end with several statements in a row that will take them closer so that everyone will end up closer to the middle. Join hands for a short prayer thanking God for fun ways to learn. End by having everyone wave his or her hands in the air and shout "Yeah God!"

Sending and Serving

7. Cards and Invitations

Activity 7 is connected to activity 8 so make sure you review activity 8 as well. Decide if you are going to invite another group for a "party" during the next session or if you want to make cards for your congregation's shut-ins, military personnel, or college students. You may have time to do both.

Gather around a table with plenty of space for the children to work. Ask them if they have ever received cards in the mail. If they have, ask them how it made them feel. Tell them that they are going to make cards for members of your church who can't come to church and so they miss seeing everyone. Make sure the children sign their first names (you may want to include their ages and a brief description of what they have drawn).

If you are making invitations to another group for the next session, be sure to include the time that the guests should come to your meeting space. As the children work, talk about what activities they might like to do or the food they would like to serve. Acknowledge all suggestions, but keep the final plans simple. When the invitations are finished, deliver them to the appropriate group. If you made cards for those who cannot attend worship, then don't forget to send them!

8. Let's Have A Party!

If you decide to do this activity, use activity 7 to create invitations that the children can send to the invitees. Coordinate with an adult, youth or children's group to come to your party.

Spend the first half of your time together decorating and preparing the snacks. If the children will be handling the food, have them clean their hands and remind them to step away from the food if they need to cough or sneeze. Assure them that they will be able to eat later and that now is not the time to sample the food.

Practice singing a song you learned in an earlier session ("Jesus Loves Me" or "Enter, Rejoice, and Come In"). Decide how you will welcome the guests (hiding and shouting surprise, standing in a line to shake hands, or some other approach). Remind the children that the guests should be allowed to sit in the chairs and that they may have to stand or sit on the floor. Also remind them that they need to thank their guests for coming and that they will need to clean up when it is time to leave.

When everyone has arrived and is seated have the children introduce themselves. Invite the guests to introduce themselves. Sing a song, say a group thank you, and serve the snacks. Encourage the children to collect and throw away any trash. As your guests leave, have your group join you at the door to shake hands with them and thank them for coming.

9. Communion Practice

For this activity you will need to educate yourself on the process of communion in your church. You might want to interview your minister to be sure that you are familiar with the format. If possible, arrange to bring the communion ware and communion elements to your home for the children to see. If this is not possible, then gather your own makeshift communion ware from items around the house.

Gather the children in your worship or story area. Begin by explaining and demonstrating for the children the format that your congregation uses for communion If possible, let them examine the communion ware and elements. Remind the children that communion is a way of remembering Jesus and connecting with other Christians. Give them the opportunity to take turns "serving" communion using communion ware. Close with a short prayer thanking God for sending Jesus to show us how to live and how to treat others.

Reflect

Think back over your time with the children.

* How has your understanding of serving others and being served changed?
* Are the children becoming more familiar with whatever rituals you use in your time together?

5

Context and Mission

Bible Focus Passages

Romans 12:9-18
Let love be genuine; hate what is evil, hold fast to what is good; love one another with mutual affection; outdo one another in showing honor. Do not lag in zeal, be ardent in spirit, serve the Lord. Rejoice in hope, be patient in suffering, persevere in prayer. Contribute to the needs of the saints; extend hospitality to strangers. Bless those who persecute you; bless and do not curse them. Rejoice with those who rejoice, weep with those who weep. Live in harmony with one another; do not be haughty, but associate with the lowly; do not claim to be wiser than you are. Do not repay anyone evil for evil, but take thought for what is noble in the sight of all. If it is possible, so far as it depends on you, live peaceably with all.

John 6:1-21
After this Jesus went to the other side of the Sea of Galilee, also called the Sea of Tiberias. A large crowd kept following him, because they saw the signs that he was doing for the sick. Jesus went up the mountain and sat down there with his disciples. Now the Passover, the festival of the Jews, was near. When he looked up and saw a large crowd coming toward him, Jesus said to Philip, "Where are we to buy bread for these people to eat?" He said this to test him, for he himself knew what he was going to do. Philip answered him, "Six months' wages would not buy enough bread for each of them to get a little." One of his disciples, Andrew, Simon Peter's brother, said to him, "There is a

boy here who has five barley loaves and two fish. But what are they among so many people?" Jesus said, "Make the people sit down." Now there was a great deal of grass in the place; so they sat down, about five thousand in all. Then Jesus took the loaves, and when he had given thanks, he distributed them to those who were seated; so also the fish, as much as they wanted. When they were satisfied, he told his disciples, "Gather up the fragments left over, so that nothing may be lost." So they gathered them up, and from the fragments of the five barley loaves, left by those who had eaten, they filled twelve baskets. When the people saw the sign that he had done, they began to say, "This is indeed the prophet who is to come into the world."

When Jesus realized that they were about to come and take him by force to make him king, he withdrew again to the mountain by himself. When evening came, his disciples went down to the sea, got into a boat, and started across the sea to Capernaum. It was now dark, and Jesus had not yet come to them. The sea became rough because a strong wind was blowing. When they had rowed about three or four miles, they saw Jesus walking on the sea and coming near the boat, and they were terrified. But he said to them, "It is I; do not be afraid." Then they wanted to take him into the boat, and immediately the boat reached the land toward which they were going.

About This Exploration

Hospitality marks the identity and inspires the action of a welcoming community. Discerning needs of the local community and expressing compassion for the global community call individuals and congregations to respond to the real need. Each individual brings unique gifts to the community and extends opportunities to share. Mission partnerships are never one-way streets. Risking outreach to others creates opportunities to receive. Feeding the hungry, clothing the naked, visiting the sick and those in prison are ways of welcoming Christ into the community. Those sent forth in mission are uniquely able to return with lessons of hospitality offered by those who have been served. Looking to God for guidance, the open hearts and serving hands that reach out to the world are the same hearts and hands that welcome.

Description of Bible Focus Passages
The immediate context of the Romans passage is Paul's exhortation to the Roman Christian community to live in the unity of Christ's spirit. In that spirit, they are to use their gifts for the common good. Love is at the top of the list, but more than just a feeling, Paul calls them to a practical love that looks for the good in others, outdo one another in showing honor, open their hearts, lives and even their homes to others. This hospitality is extended, not only to people who are receptive, but to people who persecute—to scoffers and oppressors and enemies.

The story of the feeding of the multitudes appears frequently in other gospels. However, in the gospel of John, the meal fed to the thousands is not a potluck collection of items everyone happens to have with them. The meal comes from a single donation from a youth. In the hands of the Savior, a boy's lunch is blessed and multiplied to more than adequately feed a large crowd. Who says that the simple generosity of one person cannot change the world!

Prayer
Creator God, who put within us special gifts and talents, inspire our creativity and fortify our courage so that we might continue to reach out so that others might know your grace and understand their special place in your Realm. Amen.

Deep and Wide
This book is aimed at persons who are working with younger

children ages 3-7. At this age level, children are very open and compassionate. They are quick to recognize when someone is hurting and needs help. If they can't give the help needed, they will try to get an adult involved. The flip side of this is that children this age would much rather receive than give, especially when it comes to more material objects such as toys and crayons. It is helpful for them to see and/or hear the results of their giving, even if that is a hug and thank you from their leaders when they bring in something for an outside mission.

It is easier to give out of abundance than it is out of little, but consider the words of Anne Frank: "People who give will never be poor." Watch the children as they interact with one another. Thank them for helping others, listening when someone else is talking, or working together. Think about your own need for affirmation when you give of your time or money. You may not crave public acknowledgement, but almost all of us want to know that we are making a difference in some way. Giving and receiving is a two-way street. You shouldn't do one without being willing to do the other. How graciously do you give? How graciously do you graciously receive what others to give to you no matter how small it may be?AA

Prayer
O Most Gracious God, you give to us so freely. Help me to be an example of gracious giving and receiving to these young children so that they may experience your love. Let me always be willing to share what you have given to me. Amen.

The Practices
You may want to scan the list of practices before choosing one. Doing all three activities in a group could take 90-120 minutes. Remember that young children will not be able to focus on an activity for very long. Plan more activities than you think you might need. You can always use your plan later.

Exploring and Engaging

1. Feeding the Five Thousand

For this activity, read John 6:1- 21, and gather the supplies needed to make bread and fish out of construction paper. A quick online search will help you find a template for the bread and fish if you do not feel comfortable making a template yourself. Cut enough bread and fish templates from heavy paper so that each child will have one. The children will have varying artistic abilities; be ready to praise all efforts.

If weather permits, you might take the children outside to hear the story. Gather the children in a circle and ask them to tell about a time when a lot of people came to their house to eat. Ask them the following questions:

* Who fixed the food?
* How long did it take?
* How much was there?

Now ask them to pretend that they are on a hillside listening to Jesus teach. Read them the story of Jesus feeding five thousand people or tell the story in your own words. Hand out paper, crayons, and templates. Help the children draw or trace five loaves of bread and two fish on one side of their papers. Ask how many people they think they could feed with that. Ask them to describe how many people 5,000 must be. Have them turn over their papers, or give them new ones, and ask them to draw as many people as they can in one minute. Remind them that because one child was willing to share, Jesus was able to feed even more people than they can draw.

2. Can I Help? Game

This activity is based on the principles found in Romans 12:9-18. It might be a good idea to familiarize yourself with the passage prior to the lesson.

Invite the children to sit in a line or semi-circle on the floor. Tell the children that one of them is going to act out something that a person might do. Take one child aside and give him or her an action to act out using the following list of situations:

* You are cold.
* You are hungry.
* You hurt your arm.
* You can't tie your shoe.
* You are hot.
* You are tired.
* You broke your leg.
* You broke your toy.

When they think they know how to help that person, they should raise their hand. Have the first child stand in front of the group and perform the action. Allow them to talk if they need to. When one of the other children raises a hand, invite that child to come up and help the first person. Ask the helper to explain how he or she is helping. Be sure to have the first child say "Thank you" to the helper.

Now give the second child an action to perform. Continue until all the children have had a chance to need help and to be helped. Remind the children that God wants us to help other people, even those we don't know. If it is only you and one learner then you can each take turns acting and guessing.

3. What Is Peace?
For this activity you will need a copy of *Somewhere Today: A Story of Peace* by Shelley Moore Thomas (San Val, 2001). You may be able to find it at your local library. You will also need pictures of people from many different ethnic backgrounds doing a variety of activities. Magazines and books are great resources for

pictures as are image searches on the internet.

Select music that you think of as being peaceful and have it playing as the children arrive. Gather the children in a circle and invite them to tell you what they think peace is. (Let the music continue to play.) Allow for all answers. Ask them:

* What color do you think peace is? For this age group the answer could be the same as their current favorite color, and that is okay.
* What does peace sound like? Depending on their life experience, peace may be a lack of sound.

Read the book *Somewhere Today* or another book or look at the pictures. Talk with the children about how peace can happen in small ways. Let them know that whenever we do something for or with others, we are creating a peace-filled time. Ask them to name ways they think they can help create peace. Be ready with some suggestions of your own that are specific to your group of children such as "When Bobby lets Ann help him with the puzzle" or "When Susie helped mommy with dinner..."

Discerning and Deciding

4. Thank You Cards

Think about the different volunteer positions in your congregation. With whom are the children most likely to come into contact? Are there greeters or ushers that they will see most weeks? Youth who help with the children's activities on a regular basis? Find out how many volunteers there are and decide if the children will be able to make individual cards or one or two large cards that can be displayed to show their appreciation.

Gather up heavy paper on which to make cards along with colors, markers, stickers, and whatever else you have that might help make appealing cards.

Once the lesson begins, talk with the children about the volunteers you have identified. Ask them if they know who these people are and what they do in the church. If they don't have a good grasp of the position, then fill in with any information you have. Tell them how these volunteers are showing hospitality to them and to others who come to your church.

Remind them that everyone likes to be thanked when they do something, but that we sometimes forget to thank people for the things they do. Tell them that today they are going to make thank you cards for those volunteers. Help them write "Thank You to our " (ushers, greeters, youth, whatever is appropriate) on the cards and then let them decorate it however they would like.

Be sure they sign their first names. You might want to include their ages. If possible have the children deliver the cards to the intended recipients. Or, you could present the cards during a service of worship. Lead the children in a short prayer thanking God for these volunteers and the work that they do.

5. Girl with Pineapples

Perform a simple Internet image search to locate a copy of the poster *Vendedora de Pinas* and spend time studying it. Read 1Peter 4:1-11 and look at the picture again. Does this change your reactions to the picture in any way? Use your meditation to help focus your thoughts on the activity. You will also need a whole fresh pineapple and a cut-up pineapple.

Gather the children where they can all comfortably sit and view the picture. Tell them you are going to spend one minute just looking at the picture. Then ask them how the picture makes them feel. Allow for all answers. If they haven't mentioned how the girl in the picture might be feeling, ask them what they think. Explain to them that the girl has probably helped to grow and pick the pineapples and is now trying to sell them in order to make money to buy food.

Show the children the pictures of pineapple fields and the

whole fresh pineapple. Encourage them to touch it very carefully.

Ask if they would like to walk through all those pineapple plants to take care of them and to cut the pineapples when they are ripe. Also talk about what it would be like to sit in the sun at the side of a dusty road all day trying to sell pineapples. Ask if this is something that they would like to do. Remind them that there are people who do grow pineapples just so that we can have this delicious fruit to eat.

Show them on a globe where pineapples come from (they originated in Brazil and Paraguay, but are also grown in Hawaii and Australia). Enjoy a fresh pineapple snack together, but first say a prayer thanking God for people who grow pineapples. Ask God to bless them and be with them.

6. Is There Enough?
For this activity you will need enough play dough so that each learner can have a substantial amount. Prior to the children's arrival, divide the play dough into snack-sized closeable-top bags. Have one bag out for easy access (depending on the number of children you have, this bag should only have enough dough for each child to have a marble sized piece), have a second bag hidden where the children won't come across it, and keep the rest in a bag or box out of sight.

Gather the children around a table and get out the first bag of play dough. Start to play with it and then realize that everyone else may want some too. Divide the play dough among all the children, but of course it won't be very much. Suggest that maybe you should just put it away since there really isn't enough for everyone to have a nice amount to play with.

As you begin to collect up the dough say, "What do you think (child's name)?" After they respond, bring out the second bag and ask the children if they think there will be enough to use if you combine the two bags. Acknowledge all answers, but then bring out the rest of the play dough and give each child a bag.

As they play, talk about sharing. Ask if they would rather have no play dough, just a little, or enough. Remind them of Bible story of the little boy who gave up the little amount of bread and fish he had so that everyone could have a lot of food, even leftovers.

Sending and Serving

7. Food Pantry Visitor

As this activity is about showing hospitality to strangers, spend a few minutes talking with your local food pantry. Inquire about how the pantry works, who it serves, and the kind of supplies needed.

Remind the children that you have been talking about how Jesus fed a large crowd and that it is an example of how the Bible tells us to share with others. Talk about the idea of poverty and summarize your conversation with the food pantry representative.

Read Romans 12:12-13 to the children and talk with them about how they can show hospitality to strangers by bringing food donations. Give each child a paper bag and invite them to decorate the bag. Leave the bags in a safe place to be used for activity 8.

8. How Much Food?

For this activity you will be delivering foods items to the food pantry. Recall your conversation with the food pantry and purchase enough of the needed items so that each child can place a few items in his or her lunch bag.

Have each learner create cards and drawings to hand out to the families who come to the food pantry. You can also have the children blow a kiss into a bag to help "collect love for others."

Have the children help you sort through the food, count how

much you have, talk about what you would use to make a meal. Is there anything missing? Distribute all the items in the bags along with the cards and pictures.

Form a circle around the box. Hold hands and have the children repeat the following prayer (or create one of your own): Loving God, bless this food. Let it help other children to grow strong and not be hungry. We are glad that we can help others. Amen. To end the activity, drive the children to the food pantry to deliver the food.

9. Prayers and Placemats

This activity focuses on how Jesus gave thanks to God before feeding the crowd of people (John 6:11a). Print out several different mealtime prayers from the following list:

God is great. / God is good,
God is good. / God is great,
Let us thank God / Let us thank God
For our food. / For our plate.
Amen / Amen
—(Source unknown)

For each new morning with its light,
For rest and shelter of the night,
For health and food, for love and friends,
For everything Your goodness sends.
—Ralph Waldo Emerson

Come, Lord Jesus, Be our guest. Let this food to us be blessed. Amen.
—Traditional

Praise God from whom all blessings flow;
Praise God all creatures here below;

Praise God above, you heavenly host:
Praise Father, Son, and Holy Ghost
Amen.
— Doxology

Oh, the Lord is good to me,
And so I thank the Lord,
For giving me the things I need,
The sun and the rain and the apple seed.
(Yes, the Lord is good to me.)
—Johnny Appleseed Prayer

Cut them apart and arrange each one on a piece of 8 ½" x 14" or 11" x 17" paper for a placemat. Leave room on the placemat to add a prayer that the group will create. Make a copy for each child.

Gather the children around a table. Ask if anyone has a special prayer that they say before meals and affirm all responses. If the prayers printed on the placemats are different, share those with the children. Remind the children that Jesus gave thanks to God before feeding the crowd of people (John 6:11a).

As a group, create a new mealtime prayer. Be sure to include everyone's ideas. Depending on the number of children and the amount of help you have, write the prayer on each placemat or on a separate piece of paper and make copies to cut and glue into place. Invite the children to decorate their placemats.

Cover the placemats with the precut contact paper, wrapping the extra around to the back of the placemat. If there is time, try out the placemats and the group's prayer by having a snack.

Reflect

* In your time with the children were you able to give out of abundance, from little, or from both?

* Were the children able to experience a sense of helping others within the group and outside of it?

6

Future and Vision

Bible Focus Passages

Luke 14:15-24
One of the dinner guests, on hearing this, said to him, "Blessed is anyone who will eat bread in the kingdom of God!" Then Jesus said to him, "Someone gave a great dinner and invited many. At the time for the dinner he sent his slave to say to those who had been invited, 'Come; for everything is ready now.' But they all alike began to make excuses. The first said to him, 'I have bought a piece of land, and I must go out and see it; please accept my apologies.' Another said, 'I have bought five yoke of oxen, and I am going to try them out; please accept my apologies.' Another said, 'I have just been married, and therefore I cannot come.' So the slave returned and reported this to his master. Then the owner of the house became angry and said to his slave, 'Go out at once into the streets and lanes of the town and bring in the poor, the crippled, the blind, and the lame.' And the slave said, 'Sir, what you ordered has been done, and there is still room.' Then the master said to the slave, 'Go out into the roads and lanes, and compel people to come in, so that my house may be filled. For I tell you, none of those who were invited will taste my dinner.'"

Mark 10:13-16
People were bringing little children to him in order that he might touch them; and the disciples spoke sternly to them. But when Jesus saw this, he was indignant and said to them, "Let the little children come to me; do not stop them; for it is to such as these

that the kingdom of God belongs. Truly I tell you, whoever does not receive the kingdom of God as a little child will never enter it." And he took them up in his arms, laid his hands on them, and blessed them.

About This Exploration

Pursuing hospitality invites self-examination and even criticism. Where are we as individuals and where is the community in the complexity of protecting, tending and making space for self, God, others and all creation? Where are the points of giving and receiving hospitality? How do we discover the courage to reach beyond the familiar? What growth is required as individuals and as a community? What practices, events and experiences are worthy of celebration? What sustains a continuing journey? Living into God's future calls forth a dance of individual and communal points of view, commitments, passions and understandings. God welcomes all into this future.

Deep and Wide
This book is aimed at persons who are working with younger children ages 3-7. Children this age are still fairly self-centered. They are more aware of what they want than how that will affect others. They do not think about how turning down an invitation or refusing an offer of help will hurt the other person's feelings. But they also know what it is like to be excluded from a group or an activity. Sometimes there are valid reasons for this exclusion that have to do with health, safety, or age-appropriateness, but at other times the exclusion is from their peers or because adults don't want to take the time or make the effort to include young children in an activity.

As you begin your preparation for this session pray for each child who will be in your group and for yourself. Prepare your space so that it will be welcoming to young children; include a worship/story area. As you spend time with the scripture passages think about the similarities they have. Both are about accepting those who are normally excluded.

Where do you spend your time and energy? Who receives your invitations, offers of help and support? Are you reaching out in a variety of ways to a variety of God's people? No one expects you to give up everything or solve all the problems, but have you fallen into comfortable habits with the way you reach out to others so that they know God's love? Could you stretch yourself a little more by volunteering in a soup kitchen or at a nursing home? Is there a mission project that you could help organize? You are already showing the young children that they are important by spending time with them. How can you help them see the importance of others?AA

Prayer
God of us all, help me in my daily struggle as I try not to exclude those you would invite to your great banquet. Amen.

The Practices
You may want to scan the list of practices before choosing one. Doing all three activities in a group could take 90-120 minutes. Remember that young children will not be able to focus on an activity for very long. Plan more activities than you think you might need. You can always use your plan later.

Exploring and Engaging

1. Jesus and the Children
To prepare for this activity, read Mark 10:13-16, and spend time thinking about how to make the children in your group feel welcomed and cared for. As you begin to make preparations, gather as many pictures of you can of Jesus with children. Children's Bibles and the internet can be a great resource for this.

You will also need the lyrics to the children's song "Jesus Loves Me." Bonus: Can you locate costumes to help the children reenact the Mark 10 passage? In addition, try to find a picture of *Christ among the Children* by Emil Nolde. You can either purchase a poster print of the painting or have the children view the painting on a computer screen.

Gather the children in your worship/story area. If you were able to locate pictures of Jesus with children, show these to the children and talk about how the pictures make them feel. Read Mark 10:13-16 and invite their response. Let them act out the story, using the costumes if you have them available. You may need to give them prompts the first time through.

After several repetitions, invite the children to sit in a circle. Ask them how they feel when they are told they are too little to do something. Listen carefully to their answers and point out that sometimes there are health and safety reasons for not allowing them do something like staying up late or riding a roller coaster. Do tell them that they will always be an important part of God's family.

Place your hand on the shoulder of the child to your right and say "Remember (name), God loves you." Have the children pass this blessing around the circle. End your time together by singing "Jesus Loves Me."

2. Welcome to God's Party Mural

Gather the children in your worship or story area and read aloud Luke 14:15-24. Ask:

* Have you ever had a party and invited a friend who couldn't come?
* How did that make you feel?
* Did you have time to invite someone else?

Tell them that God is having a party and everyone is invited, not just a few people. Explain that some people don't understand about God, so they have turned down the invitation. But God isn't giving up; they are still invited. Also let them know that since they want to learn about Jesus, they have said "Yes" to God's invitation. (They won't understand all this yet, but you are planting seeds that will grow.)

Ask them what they think God's party looks like and who is there. Move to a table and invite them to create a picture of God's party. If you are using one large piece of paper, assign different parts for them to draw. Be sure they sign their names to their creation. Add a title and the scripture reference. You may want to write a brief explanation under each section of the mural. Display the mural the next time you meet with the children.

3. Not a Straight Path Painting

As the group leader, spend some time thinking about your personal faith journey. Has it been a straight path? More than likely the answer is no. There have been some twists, turns, and backtracking along the way. But God is still there with open arms. Our lives are not perfect. We never know for sure how things are going to turn out, but there is still beauty to be found.

Gather the children in your worship or story area and remind them that you have been talking about hospitality and doing things for others. Ask them if it is always easy to be nice others. Let them know that even though we forget sometimes, God wants us to keep trying. Explain that you are going to make paintings that show how we don't always walk in a straight line when we follow Jesus.

If you are working with a large group of children let them know that only one or two of them paint at a time. While they wait their turn, they may read books or work puzzles. Before they paint they will need to put on a smock or paint shirt. Before each child paints, write the child's name on the paper. When they are finished, put the paintings in a safe place to dry. Feel free to choose from either Option 1 or 2 for this activity.

Option 1: Fold a piece of paper in half and open it back up. Choose one color of paint. Pick the string up out of the paint by the clean end and lay it on one side of the paper in a wiggle pattern with the clean end off the edge of the paper. Fold the top half of the paper over and hold it down lightly while the child pulls out the string. Return the string to the paint. Open the paper to see the design.

Option 2: Place the piece of paper in a shoebox with the ends of the paper rolling up the sides. Pick 2 or 3 paint colors. Use a spoon to roll a marble around in the paint to coat it. Then place the painted marbles in the shoebox, and put on the lid. Let the child shake the shoebox side-to-side and front to back. Remove the lid, remove the marbles and the paper, and enjoy the design.

Discerning and Deciding

4. New and Used

For this lesson, spend some time thinking about the things that you give and receive prior to the arrival of the children.

* How do you feel when you are on the receiving end of only half of someone else's attention?
* How many times have you given only half of your attention to someone?
* What kinds of things have you given to charity or to thrift stores?
* How do you want the items you buy to look?
* Think about the different economic levels from which the children in your group come. Is it possible to have your group do a short-term toy or book collection for a local homeless or children's shelter?

Gather the children in your worship or story area and show them two toys, one in a brand new box and one old. Ask them which they would rather have. Most children will go with the newer item. Ask them why they would pick that one rather than the other. Use the following questions to lead them in a simple discussion:

- * How would they feel if someone gave them an old toy?
- * Would they want to keep it or give it back?
- * Ask if they have ever sorted through their own toys and given some away. Were the things they gave away still good to play with, or were they worn out?
- * Do they think other children would have really wanted them?

Remind the children that sometimes people who don't have very much are more willing to share than those who have a lot because they know what it is like to not have enough. Lead the children in a prayer thanking God for all that they do have and asking for help to be kind and generous to others.

If time allows, drive the children to a local helper and drop off the new toy.

5. Water, Water, Everywhere?
For this activity you will need to locate a copy of the picture *The Public Fountain* by Manual Alvarez Bravo and spend some time studying the print. If you cannot find a hardcopy then perform an internet search to pull up the image. Use the following questions as you meditate on the poster:

- * Where do you think this young boy lives?
- * Is this his only source of water?
- * Is there running water in his home?
- * Think about your own situation and that of the children in your group. How might it be different from this boy's

situation?
* Read Luke 14:15-24. Would this boy have been on the first guest list or the second?

Think about all the places in your home or meeting space where you could get a drink, and map out the longest route possible to get to them. Cover each water source with an "Out of Order" sign before you begin your walk.

Gather the children where they can sit comfortably and view the hardcopy of the poster or the online image. Spend one full minute looking at it in silence. Then ask them what they think is going on in the picture using the following questions:

* How old is the boy?
* Why is he drinking from the pipe?
* Where does the water come from?
* Where is it going?
* Who else uses this well?

This picture was taken in Mexico, but it could easily have been taken in the Middle East, South America, or any number of other places. Show the children these areas on the globe. Ask the children what it would be like if they had to walk to a public well to get their water.

Tell the children that all of you are going to take a walk to get a drink. Take the long way around as much as possible to get to the first source of water. If the weather is nice you can always lead them on a roundabout outside adventure to get to the water. When it cannot be used, ask the children where you should go next. Start off again, once more taking the longest route possible. When you cannot use the next source, ask the children what to do next.

Ask them how they are feeling. Is anyone getting thirsty or tired? Trudge on to the next source of water (or back to the original site if you need to). At last everyone can get a drink, but before you do say a short prayer thanking God for the gift of clean, fresh water. After everyone has had a drink, ask the children how they feel now. Take the shortest route back to your meeting space.

6. Signs of Hospitality Walk

For this activity you will need a long rope with knots tied approximately every three feet. The rope will be used to guide the group on their hospitality walk. To help keep the children together in a group, have them hold on to the long rope as you walk around your home or the grounds of wherever it is that you are meeting. If possible, recruit a helper to assist on the walk.

Take the children on the walk. Stop at doors, tables, pictures, windows, restrooms, and so forth. At each stop ask the children:

* How would you describe this location?
* Is it difficult or hard for you to see?
* Think about those who have different physical abilities. How difficult it would be to maneuver through the space in a wheelchair or similar item?
* How do you think things could be made better?
* If weather and location permit, walk around the outside as well. Ask: Does this look friendly and nice?
* How could it be mase better?

Acknowledge all ideas that the children name.

Sending and Serving

7. What Can We Do for Others? What Can Others Do for Us?

Prior to the start of the activity, spend some time thinking about the children in your group and how they treat one another.

Consider their age differences. Are there some things that the older children can do for the younger ones? What can the younger children do for the older children?

Gather the children in a circle. Ask them to think about ways that other people help them (tying shoes, reaching something up high, spelling words for them, and so forth). Ask them to think about things that they can do for others (picking up something off the floor, setting the table, giving a hug, and so forth.) Make sure they come up with things that they can do for one another and not just for adults. Have them act out their ideas. Remind them to say "thank you" after someone "helps" them.

Give each child a piece of paper. Help them fold the paper in half and draw a line down the middle. On one side ask them to draw a picture of them helping someone. On the other side ask them to draw a picture of someone helping them. Label the pictures and put them on display.

8. "Come All You People" (Uyai Mose)

For this activity, you will need to review the words to the song "Come, All You People" (tune: Uyai Mose Iona Community), a Zimbabwe folk song. If you are not familiar with the song, it can be purchased online for a nominal fee or heard at http://www.youtube.com/watch?v=nAawJ5VzBl0

The lyrics are as follows:

> Come all you people
> Come and praise your Maker
> Come all you people
> Come and praise your Maker
> Come all you people
> Come and praise your Maker
> Come now and worship the Lord

Gather the children where they can see a map or globe. Explain that you are going to learn a song from the African country of Zimbabwe. Show them where this country is in relation to where you live. Remind the children that God's love extends to everyone in the world. Go over the song with them several times.

Explain that in many parts of Africa dried beans are used to make instruments. Distribute paper plates and invite the children to decorate the bottom side. Let them pick out several lengths of crepe paper or ribbon. Help them fold the plate in half and insert one end of the streamers at the fold. Staple the two edges of the plate together being sure to catch the ends of the streamers. Place the staples close together so that the beans won't fall out. When you are about halfway around the edge, help the children pour in a small cup of beans. Finish closing the paper plate shaker.

Sing the song again and include the following motions:

On the word "come," gesture with a hand to come.
On the words "praise your Maker," use the shakers.
On the words "worship the Lord," raise hands in the air.
Remember, have fun.

9. Welcome to God's Party Cards

As this activity involves extending welcome to people at church, it will be helpful to spend some time thinking about how others make you feel welcome when you go to their homes, or even when you come to church. To demonstrate this, the children will be making cards to hand out to church attendees. Write "Welcome to God's Party," "Thank you for coming to God's party," We are glad you came to God's party," or similar phrases on a piece of paper posted where the children can see to copy. You might want to pre-print the phrases on some or all of the cards depending on the abilities of your group.

Gather the children around your workspace and read or retell the story in Luke 14:15-24. Remind them that people who come to church have already accepted God's invitation. Now you are going to do something to make them feel welcome. Distribute the cards and show the children the phrases you have written. Explain that they are to copy the phrases and decorate the cards. Perhaps the older children could write the phrases and the younger children could decorate the cards. When they are finished, explain that on Sunday you will scatter the cards around the sanctuary or worship area for people to find. If possible, let the children help you scatter the cards. Don't forget to leave some for your music and worship team leaders.

Reflect

In your time together, have you been able to see a change in the children? Even if you are not able to see this change, don't despair. Know that you have planted seeds of love and hospitality. It may take time for these seeds to take root and sprout upward, but they are there, and you have made a difference.

Appendix

About Faith Practices

This book is based on Faith Practices (www.faithpractices.org), which is designed for groups to select and work activities together. If you are seeking a group experience tailored by you or others from a wealth of options, then we encourage you to investigate this much broader resource. This book has selected only a portion of those options—usually the ones that can be done individually.

These activities are not warmed over Sunday school lessons, but move way beyond to invite reflection, journaling, and conversation with others. This point is important. Today congregations find themselves faced with challenges to their familiar styles of education and faith formation. Since the early days of the Sunday school movement, churches used the education model, which focuses primarily on head knowledge, for religious instruction. We have held onto that schooling concept right up to today, with children still sitting around tables, still doing fill-in-the-blank worksheets and still memorizing scripture verses. You may recall this approach.

Those models no longer seem suitable, especially to younger adults, and do not necessarily fit the needs of people searching for a deeper relationship with God and Jesus Christ rather than facts and dogma. Even schools moved away from that "traditional" way of teaching as they create more interactive classrooms and rely on research related to styles of learning, multiple intelligences, and brain functioning.

New forms of ministry, in which discipleship leads to personal and communal transformation, are emerging in local churches. Many are searching for resources that will weave together what happens in worship with what happens in the church's education program. Both education and worship are changed, reformed in this approach. We believe that the language of practicing faith gives churches a vocabulary they need to describe this new world of learning, worship, and serving as they seek to be vital congregations.

The scholarship of Dorothy Bass and her colleagues around practicing our faith spurred a growing conversation that focuses on deepening one's relationship with God through shared activities that form a way of discipleship, a way of Christian living. While many understand practicing the faith to be an individual pursuit, we affirm that communities of faith develop patterns of living that reflect their faith. Practicing our faith is both personal and public. "Faith development does not occur in a vacuum, but rather is cultivated intentionally by a community of faith-filled people" (Woolever and Bruce, *Beyond the Ordinary: 10 Strengths of U.S. Congregations*, p. 55).

Living out the faith, exercising our faith, practicing our faith is a lifelong process. At every turn and in every stage of life, the stories of our biblical heritage take on new meaning, our relationship with God grows and changes, and discernment about our life's journey shifts and transforms as a result of both our physical and our spiritual maturation.

Many lists of faith practices, some ancient and some contemporary, are available. Through a process of group discernment, twelve circles of practices for congregations to immerse themselves were identified. These seek a deeper, stronger relationship with God through Jesus Christ and the Holy Spirit and with one another. This series is not linearly progressive, not chronological, and not organized by the church year or calendar. None of the practices of faith are exclusive to any one circle. Some fit easily into several circles. These faith practices are not practiced in isolation; they relate to one another.

Nine Characteristics of Christian Practices

Each Christian practice of faith:
Involves us in God's activities in the world and reflects God's grace and love
Is a complex set of acts, words, and images that addresses one area of fundamental need
Is learned with and from other people
Comes to us from the past and will be shaped by us for the future
Is thought-full; it implies certain beliefs about ourselves, our neighbors, and God
Is done within the church, in the public realm, in daily work, and at home
Shapes the people who participate in the practice, individually and communally
Has good purposes, although it often becomes corrupted
Comes to focus in worship (www.practingourfaith.org, used by permission)

These statements create a framework out of which the components are developed. Thus, this section of the Foundations Paper will continue to emerge throughout the development of the resource.)

Faith Practice Affirmations

The following theological principles have guided our work. You may want to check these against your own faith understanding:

We believe in God, the Eternal Spirit, who is made known to us in Jesus our brother, and to whose deeds we testify
God calls the worlds into being, creates humankind in the divine image, and sets before us the ways of life and death

God seeks in holy love to save all people from aimlessness and sin

God judges all humanity and all nations by that will of righteousness declared through prophets and apostles

In Jesus Christ, the man of Nazareth, our crucified and risen Lord, God has come to us and shared our common lot, conquering sin and death and reconciling the whole creation to its Creator

God bestows upon us the Holy Spirit, creating and renewing the church of Jesus Christ, binding in covenant faithful people of all ages, tongues, and races

God calls us into the church to accept the cost and joy of discipleship, to be servants in the service of the whole human family, to proclaim the gospel to all the world and resist the powers of evil, to share in Christ's baptism and eat at his table, to join him in his passion and victory

God promises to all who trust in the gospel forgiveness of sins and fullness of grace, courage in the struggle for justice and peace, the presence of the Holy Spirit in trial and rejoicing, and eternal life in that kingdom which has no end

Seek to participate in God's mission and to follow the way of the crucified and risen Christ.

Empowered by the Holy Spirit, we are called and commit ourselves to:

Praise God, confess our sin, and joyfully accept God's forgiveness

Proclaim the Gospel of Jesus Christ in our suffering world

Embody God's Love for all people

Hear and give voice to creation's cry for justice and peace

Name and confront the powers of evil within and among us

Repent our silence and complicity with the forces of chaos and death

Preach and teach with the power of the living Word

Join oppressed and troubled people in the struggle for liberation

Work for justice, healing, and wholeness of life

Embrace the unity of Christ's church

Discern and celebrate the present and coming reign of God

These educational practices are also exhibited in the activities suggested:

Collaboration is essential to "equip the saints for the work of ministry, for building up the body of Christ" (Ephesians 4:12).

Involvement of the whole church community is not only invited, but imperative in creating the resources.

The use of scripture is fundamental.

Scripture from both the Old and New Testaments will be used in each practice

Scripture selection is not confined to the lectionary

We will use inclusive language in our presentation of the texts

Scripture will be used as a catalyst for helping learners explore the faith

Scripture is both formative and informative

No text is exclusive to any one practice – one text can open up many practices

We will not proof text, but will use verses in context

Scripture will be selected that is appropriate to each age level

There are many styles of learning, and there are multiple intelligences.

The role of the leader is to be a pilgrim guide.

The community of faith is transformative.

Learners of all ages need opportunities to experience practices of faith individually and in community, not just to engage in academic study.

Art is used to open up reflection, not to illustrate a text.

Portrayals of diversity include examples, stories, art, music, names, settings, rituals, and traditions that represent the world in its fullness: diversity of cultures, backgrounds, abilities, orientation, classes, and race. While these may be visible differences, we acknowledge there are also invisible diversities, such as learning disabilities.

We honor the ability of all learners to be interpreters of the faith and the stories of faith.

Circle Books

Circle is a symbol of infinity and unity. It's part of a growing list of imprints, including o-books.net and zero-books.net.

Circle Books aims to publish books in Christian spirituality that are fresh, accessible, and stimulating.

Our books are available in all good English language bookstores worldwide. If you can't find the book on the shelves, then ask your bookstore to order it for you, quoting the ISBN and title. Or, you can order online—all major online retail sites carry our titles.

To see our list of titles, please view www.Circle-Books.com, growing by 80 titles per year.

Authors can learn more about our proposal process by going to our website and clicking on Your Company > Submissions.

We define Christian spirituality as the relationship between the self and its sense of the transcendent or sacred, which issues in literary and artistic expression, community, social activism, and practices. A wide range of disciplines within the field of religious studies can be called upon, including history, narrative studies, philosophy, theology, sociology, and psychology. Interfaith in approach, Circle Books fosters creative dialogue with non-Christian traditions.

And tune into MySpiritRadio.com for our book review radio show, hosted by June-Elleni Laine, where you can listen to authors discussing their books.